THE CLIMATE TRIBUNAL

INDEX

Foreword

This publication presents a collection of texts and research by Paolo Cirio on his activist and artistic work addressing climate change.

The *Climate Tribunal* aims to shift perception of both the general public and cultural producers by exposing historical, scientific, political-economic, and criminal evidence of how the fossil fuel industry is accountable for having caused climate change. The reflections provided explore the ethics of representation of climate change, as well as pressing concerns in adapting and reacting to a new cultural and social reality.

The *Climate Tribunal* is a rhetorical device to discuss how the fossil fuel industry not only obstructs social justice, but also knowledge, literacy, and discourse. While the fossil fuel economy causes climate emergencies, it also generates misrepresentation, misconception, and misuse of cultural and artistic works addressing climate change. With the *Climate Tribunal*, the ethics of climate change range from responsibility for inequalities and injustice, to the ethics of culturally engaging with these topics. The essays, research, and interventions by Paolo Cirio aim to provide reflection and knowledge for journalists, artists, curators, philosophers, activists, and anyone communicating and engaging in culture around climate change.

Alongside aesthetic and ethical reflections, artistic works and scientific studies, this book includes research by Paolo Cirio on the historical role of the fossil fuel economy in causing climate change and derailing climate policy. This historical evidence is integrated into the new forensic discipline of Attribution Science, which is able to establish links between climate anomalies and greenhouse emissions. Cirio combines this evidence to advance climate justice and cultural public engagement through advocacy in Climate Litigation.

Through the concept of the *Climate Tribunal*, Cirio aims to shift cultural perspectives on the responsibility for the current climate and ecological crisis, focusing on the real culprits that remain unpunished, instead of blaming citizens. For this debunking, Cirio examines economics, geopolitics, and histories to represent and understand the century of the fossil fuel regime, as well as the rhetoric and aesthetics that legitimated it though soft power in politics and culture.

In addition to the artistic work of Paolo Cirio, his activist work includes the campaign *Climate Class Action* launched in 2023, and can be traced back to his first climate justice project in New York City in 2010. Cirio's activism also touches on the responsibility of the cultural sector, through direct critique of art institutions. Ultimately, Cirio advocates for a more effective Climate Aesthetics that might integrate the politics, economics, and ethics of the current epochal planetary emergency.

All texts in this publication have been written by Paolo Cirio, who prefers to write in third person to make it a research project rather than a personal statement.

Introduction to the Climate Tribunal

The *Climate Tribunal* is a conceptual framework to discuss the cultural perception and representation of climate change. These cultural conceptions relate to the fields of knowledge, aesthetics, and ethics, which are examined in the critical analysis by Paolo Cirio in this publication.

The *Climate Tribunal* intends to persecute climate crimes committed by fossil fuel companies and those who supported them. These crimes include the creation of misleading semiotics, rhetorics, and morals that for decades polluted the cultural world and consequently public opinion regarding climate change. The Climate Aesthetics of the *Climate Tribunal* focuses on social science to present evidence that can bring climate justice, realist perspective, and new knowledge, moving beyond the notion of the Capitalocene[1] and the Anthropocene[2]. As such, the *Climate Tribunal* is a cultural device that looks at aesthetics and ethics as tools for social justice.

Alongside critical theory and investigation of evidence against fossil fuel companies, the *Climate Tribunal* also takes the form of public art and activism. Paolo Cirio created a body of work on climate justice, which includes activist campaigns, such as *Extinction Claims*, *Flooding NYC Claims*, and in particular the *Climate Class Action*. This creative use of the law as art material refers to the concept of 'Legal Imagination'[3] and what Cirio defines as 'Regulatory Art'[4], where artists creatively propose legal vehicles and frameworks.

A *Climate Tribunal* should be established to investigate atrocities committed by those involved in the fossil fuel industry. For instance, CEOs of private enterprises should be seen as war criminals that have committed climate crimes[5]. A Nuremberg-style trial to prosecute climate criminals could achieve justice for the crimes committed, as well as sentencing compensations and reparations for victims. These crimes have been indiscriminate, and today they even seem intentional. Currently, there are dozens of lawsuits against fossil fuel companies, so far none as crimes as against humanity, however some legal theories are already considering the crime of murder[6], while some look toward other legal bodies like the International Criminal Court (ICC), or seek special jurisdictions based on the number of deaths caused by climate change[7]. So far, current lawsuits mainly seek financial compensations for local governments, states, or cities, which would use the funds to adapt to climate change. As the world begins to witness mass displacement, mortality, and destruction, it can be questioned if the fossil fuel industry knowingly was aiming for disruptions to weaken society, making it even more dependent on fossil fuels and leading to an authoritarian political future[8]. After all, the fossil fuels industry had knowledge of the consequences and their economic interests often aligned with authoritarian political interests.

In the artworks created for the *Climate Tribunal*, Cirio accuses the major oil, gas, and coal companies with data, photos, graphs, and documents on climate change. Highlighted prints with data, photos, texts, and graphics are presented as evidence. Plaintiffs and defendants are included in the form of artworks. Climate crisis experts intervene as witnesses and audiences participate as jury or as injured party. Cirio's visuals feature scientific and economic data, legal documents, geopolitical analysis, biological studies, and satellite images. The *Climate Tribunal* aims to support vulnerable citizens, endangered natural species, and damaged ecosystems to seek financial compensation from those who have caused the climate crisis on a massive scale. Informed by climate change litigation cases, ecocide bills, and global climate treaties, for this tribunal, Paolo Cirio combines Attribution Science with the legal concept of 'environmental personhood', and the 'right of nature' jurisprudential theory.

In the *Climate Tribunal*, "the concept of sovereignty is extended to the natural world and envisions a future in which human beings, natural species and ecosystems acquire supranational rights codified by international public laws. The future climate policy will not only have to include a transition to more sustainable economies; it will ultimately require rebuilding economic, social, and natural systems from climate disasters, and holding those who have caused damage of unprecedented proportions accountable for their actions"[9].

Central to Cirio's concept is the historical study Carbon Major Database by the Climate Accountability Institute, the first that established precise responsibilities each international fossil fuel firm has. The top 100 major oil, gas, and coal producers have generated over 70% of greenhouse gas emissions[10], making them the greatest threat to human society, ecosystems, and their endangered species. Most of these companies have also been spreading misinformation and obstructing knowledge about the role of their products and activities in causing climate change. In particular, western companies were aware to begin with, and yet decided to expand in other parts of the world. The political-economic historic evidence can be combined with scientific evidence of causes and effects of climate change to sentence the fossil fuel companies to pay for their crimes.

In this publication the *Climate Tribunal* expands to critical theory, scientific considerations, legal prepositions, and political economic history.

Notes

1. The term Capitalocene, coined by Jason W. Moore, describes the current geological epoch, highlighting the influence of capitalism on the earth's ecosystems and climate.

2. The term Anthropocene was widely popularized in 2000 by atmospheric chemist Paul J. Crutzen, who regards the influence of human behavior on earth's atmosphere in recent centuries as so significant as to constitute a new geological epoch.

3. "Legal imagination shows that environmental law involves the deliberate development of legal systems to respond to the complexity of environmental problems while ensuring the stability of legal systems. Legal imagination is needed to develop law to respond to a world of multiple interconnected parties and socio-political conflict." From "Environmental Law: A Very Short Introduction" book by Elizabeth Fisher.

4. "This art addresses, envisions, and practices regulation when institutions fail to fairly regulate the fields that constitute society such as trade, labor, healthcare, technology, media, education, and the environment." From "Regulatory Art" text by Paolo Cirio, 2018.

5. "The problem with emissions of greenhouse gas is that the harm they do is not paid for. Justice requires that, when people suffer harm, they should be compensated for them. [...] The harm is not accidental. That strengthens the duty on us to make restitution. [...] An injustice is not only necessarily canceled by compensation. It is plausible that people have rights to specific goods, such as an unpolluted environment." From "Climate Matters, Ethics in a Warming World" book by John Broome, 2012.

6. "New climate paper calls for charging big U.S. oil firms with homicide". From The Guardian, March 2023.

7. "How to set a value on human lives. Climate change will kill people in various ways. It will do so through climate disasters such as floods, storms, droughts, and heat waves. It will increase the range of diseases; it will make it harder to feed the world's population, and cause famines; it will drastically damage water supplies, and perhaps lead to wars." From "Climate Matters, Ethics in a Warming World" book by John Broome, 2012.

8. "One of the things we know about crises is that often people use crises as an opportunity to grab power, and so I do think that as climate change proceeds, and we see more and more damage, and the damage becomes more and more frightening, that the risk to liberal democracy will be very, very great." By Naomi Oreskes from the interview on the podcast Knowable Magazine, 2022.

9. "The concept of justice will evolve into a larger interconnected system, in which natural species, ecosystems and humans may constitute themselves as climate victims, while corporate and political entities will be identified as criminals." From "Natural Sovereignty" text by Paolo Cirio, 2021.

10. "Just 100 companies responsible for 71% of global emissions". In 2017, The Carbon Majors Report pinpointed "how a relatively small set of fossil fuel producers may hold the key to systemic change on carbon emissions," says Pedro Faria, technical director at environmental non-profit Carbon Disclosure Project (CDP), which published the report in collaboration with the Climate Accountability Institute. From The Guardian, July 2017.

Accountability

"What individuals can do to stop global warming?
Nothing." [1]

The *Climate Tribunal* is a cultural device to reframe the accountability concerning climate change. Who's to blame and who pays for it, these ethical concerns have been generalized with the universalizing rhetoric of mainstream environmentalism, which tends to hold everyone equally responsible and vulnerable to climate change[2]. In particular, a common misconception is that individuals alone are accountable for global warming, rather than considering the accountability of specific economic and political factors.

In the media, academia, culture, and politics, the misrepresentation around responsibility has been built around several cultural aspects, such as a simple lack of literacy, but also malicious deception, secrecy, and censorship, or with strategic use of semiotic and linguistic devices for the making of false morals[3], and also twisting hard science and economics. The following analysis briefly gives some more context for some of these factors that made climate change too often misrepresented and misunderstood. For instance climate change should not be seen as a scientific problem, but an economic one. It should not be measured in terms of increase of temperature, but in the amount of barrels of oil traded and quantity of other fossil fuels produced yearly, as well as the number of pipelines built and tanks crossing the oceans.

In the *Climate Tribunal*, accountability centers on the emissions of greenhouse gasses produced by fossil fuel corporations, who intentionally spread misinformation about climate change and mislead politicians for decades. Some might argue that citizens caused emissions to spike by consuming the fossil fuels that were produced by those companies. However, citizens had no option to choose different energy systems, and were not informed properly about these important decisions society needed to address. Instead citizens were forced to use fossil fuel by creating more dependency and demand for it. Obviously, the fossil fuel producers prioritized selling more of their products and maximizing profit, while citizens did not have the means for alternatives. Some might argue that politicians should be the ones held accountable for not having implemented legislation to curb the use of fossil fuels. However, politicians easily fell prey to the influence of the industry, which corrupts politics in several forms. Some could argue that international institutions should take the blame. However, those institutions are governed by the same industry and politics that kept misinforming citizens about the consequences of burning fossil fuels.

Some hold the belief that the accountability rests with the Anthropocene, a very simplistic analysis, sometimes in response there are those who argue that Capitalism is to blame, using the concept of the Capitalocene. However, Capitalism would still exist with nuclear and renewable energy. Technically, everything would refer to the Industrial Revolution or consumerism in particular, which expanded the production of fossil fuels. Coincidentally, this particular product is also the main means of exchange and the main instrument of power of the current human civilization. Thus, rather than just Capitalism, Imperialism could be blamed, something that can be explained by geopolitics, also considering that Russia, Iran, and Venezuela account for about 40% of nationalized oil fields, and China, as a large producer, is also the largest Communist country[4], and yet the U.S. military is the largest institutional consumer of oil in the world.

Without getting into macroeconomics, arguments about accountability can be based on historical facts and evidence, therefore investigating specific named individuals who have made concrete decisions and taken concrete action to deceive society and influence political decision making. Among the large consumers and producers of fossil fuel there are some that have played a more significant role, and those live in impunity. For example, this is the case of Exxon's CEOs who intentionally manipulated public opinion and political debates. And among countries and populations, the United States has an enormous responsibility regarding historical production and consumption of fossil fuels, and has exported an economic model based on oil elsewhere, for its own interest. Nevertheless, a few specific politicians supported these companies and economies despite being aware of the consequences, making them particularly responsible as well.

In conclusion, the reality about accountability over climate change is often misunderstood and misrepresented. Culture and art have the duty to create new knowledge and challenge the normative narrative that in our epoch is driven by disinformation, green-washing, and ethics-washing. Critical art can enhance cultural perception to raise awareness on climate change accountability, shifting it from having individuals feel responsible to holding major fossil fuel firms accountable.

Notes

1. "The hard truth is that the answer to the question 'What can I, as an individual, do to stop climate change?' is: nothing. You can't do anything. In fact, the very idea that we, as atomized individuals, even lots of anatomized individuals, could play a significant part in stabilizing the planet's climate system or changing the global economy is objectively nuts. Only a massive and organized movement can do that." From "On Fire" book by Naomi Klein, 2019.

2. 50 percent of global emissions are produced by the richest 10 percent of the population; the wealthiest 20 percent are responsible for the 70 percent. This creates a large 'climate debt', which bigger emitters owe to poorer countries.

3. "The detailed analysis will rely on the quantitative methods of economics, but its underlying principles must be based on ethics. We as citizens need to make our own judgments about these ethical principles in order to participate responsibly in the democratic process." From "Climate Matters, Ethics in a Warming World" book by John Broome, 2012.

4. Only from 2006, China overtook the U.S. to become the world's largest annual emitter of greenhouse gasses and its citizens now have carbon footprints well above the global average. However, its cumulative and per-capita emissions remain about half of the United States' today.

Annual Emissions of Carbon Dioxide (Gigatons)

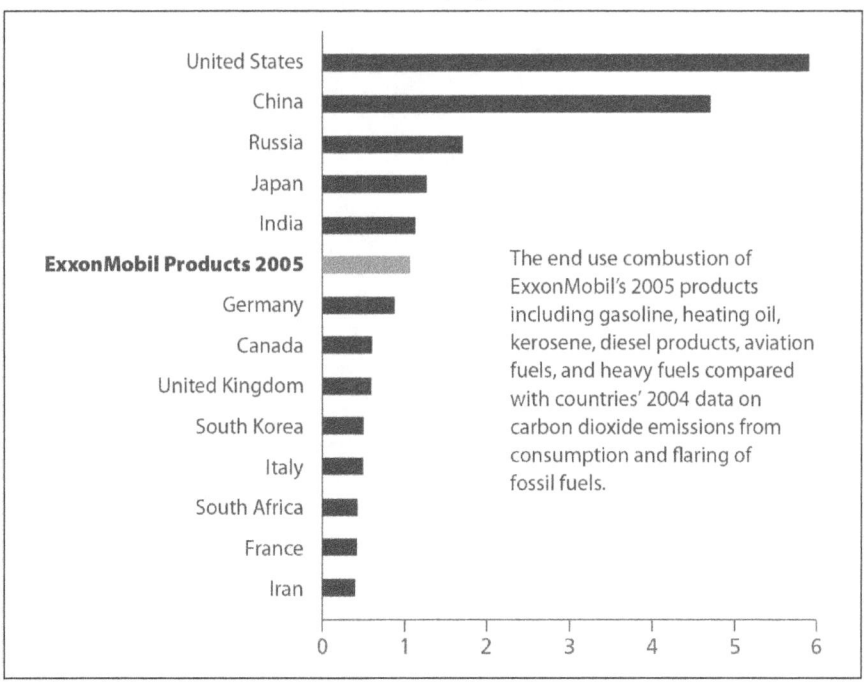

The end use combustion of ExxonMobil's 2005 products including gasoline, heating oil, kerosene, diesel products, aviation fuels, and heavy fuels compared with countries' 2004 data on carbon dioxide emissions from consumption and flaring of fossil fuels.

Total Emissions (Cumulative and Projected)

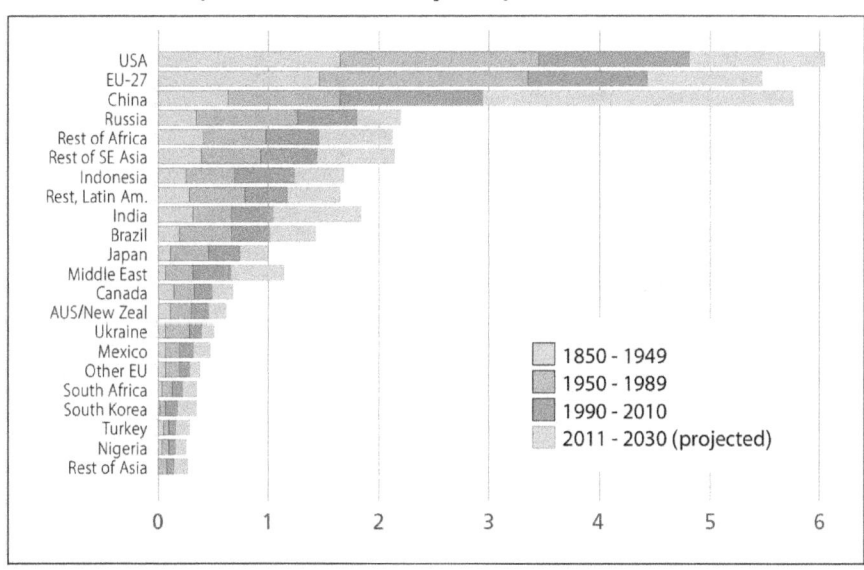

Ethics and Morals

To reflect on the ethics of climate change, it's necessary to define a difference between morals and ethics, as the use of the two words influence our understanding of responsibility for global warming. Even though in Anglo-American language the meaning of the word 'morals' is interchangeable with the meaning of 'ethics', in this context let's consider a European meaning of 'morals' as imperatives deriving from rules established by authority or religion. In contrast, let's consider the modern word 'ethics' as a dynamic science that departs from comparative analysis to achieve goodness and find resolutions for disputed injustices. These definitions should help seeing how false morals around climate change have formed.

Corporations often create new moral standards by focusing on consumers' environmental sustainability[1]. Also governments use similar moralizing strategies for citizens to avoid responsibility. For instance, the United States, Norway, and France are among the largest producers of fossil fuels, and yet morally address climate change. Unfortunately, these morals have been integrated in literature on ethics itself. In fact, most writing by both moral philosophers in the U.S. and post-structuralists in Europe often reduced the ethical problems of climate change to the morality of individuals. Unaware of the history and economics of fossil fuel industry, a general understanding is that governments hold collective responsibility for climate change[2] while individuals bear a moral responsibility through their behavior, lifestyle, and political choices[3]. This common interpretation can be found in books like "The Ethics of Climate Change", "Perfect Moral Storm. The Ethical Tragedy of Climate Change", "Climate Matters, Ethics in a Warming World", and hundreds of academic papers, most of which fail to even mention the words "fossil fuels" and the role of the corporate power in influencing culture in society.

These notions, almost as if they were dogmatic texts, made their way to universities, media, and popular culture, creating morals that often even lack rationality. Those morals became feelings that relate to judgment, which are often internalized as moralist notions of good or bad behaviors, without looking at large behavioral patterns and thus ethical analyses. These judgmental morals are then amplified by manipulative communication plans that are specifically designed to shift the focus from blaming accountable entities to judging personal morals, which eventually generates interpersonal discord and polarizes society. The history of manipulative advertising regarding environmental damage goes back to the famous 'Crying Indian' commercial, in 1970, made by the polluting packaging industry to avoid regulations and instead blaming individuals for littering. It was then the idea of the 'Carbon Footprint' by British Petroleum (BP) that moralized personal ethics of climate change. In 2004, the company unveiled its "carbon footprint calculator" to make citizens responsible for global warming by making them asses their daily life as going to work, buying food, and traveling[4]. Later this strategy advanced with the idea of the green consumer, promising that ethical shopping could ward off climate change. For instance, in 2007, both Chevron and Philips Electronics promoted replacing fluorescent light bulb as a meaningful way for consumers to save the planet[5]. The communication strategy of green consumerism is today the mainstream one, we can make right moral decisions by buying anything that is already marked as the right 'green choice', even when buying flights or plastic goods. Today the industry certifies our moral choice through labeling it directly on the product.

Nevertheless, this still implies being able to afford to buy and consume sustainably, or having the luxury to be ethical, given for the majority of people in the world, no such choice exists, they only suffer due to a disproportional freedom of choice on behalf of wealthier individuals[6]. Even that freedom is actually very limited by keeping all individuals dependent on an economic system based on fossil fuel for a global trade that relies on manufacturing in countries where labor is cheap, to be quickly consumed in the wealthier part of the planet. The ethics of climate change can vary greatly, from a geographical and temporal point of view. For instance, greenhouse emissions doubled since the beginning of globalization, as global trade agreements allowing a free market accelerated manufacturing, shipping, and traveling around the world. These emissions have accumulated slowly over decades and will remain in the atmosphere for centuries. We will see their effects much later, and often in parts of the world we would never set foot in. Personal responsibility can relate to personal ethics, however the current global economic system was designed to have billions of people in an inescapable global consumerist lifestyle, almost as an anthropological condition of an entire world civilization based on massive fossil fuel consumption. In fact, the global trade of resources and goods make everything connected to the economy of fossil fuels. For example, a simple cotton T-Shirt[7], even one made from natural material, requires being grown, manufactured, packaged, and shipped using fossil fuel machinery and chemicals.

With all due respect for personal ethics, the reality of our contemporary global economy has little to do with moral imperatives, where different choices may be noble, but ultimately ineffective in tackling climate change. While it is considered immoral for an individual to take flights for work, hundreds of millions travel for mindless tourism. While having a vegetarian diet is a moral imperative, the meat industry shows uncontrolled growth. While it's a moral decision to buy an electric car, it's not addressed how many barrels of oil are needed to produce all new electric cars. The chains of overconsumption remain unchecked and it's a privilege to make such moral decisions, as the majority of the population in the world can't afford the same, and eventually they are shamed by those who claim to be morally superior.

The science of ethics would instead consider what are scientifically the right choices, focusing on power relations that are causing the climate crisis, and social inequalities that determine its uneven effects. The ethics of climate change regarding limiting further emissions can only be measured in radical actions against consumerist society and the fossil fuel industry. Like the fight by social movements to change policy-making or even directly block airports, roads, and banks, disrupting the production and trade of fossil fuel and its mass consumption. These actions, even if still symbolic, are scientifically and ethically the only rational and logical ethics individuals can embrace to tackle climate change[8]. What remains highly unethical is to misrepresent and ignore this reality[9].

References

James Garvey explores individual responsibility in book "The Ethics of Climate Change: Right and Wrong in a Warming World", Bloomsbury publishing, 2008.

Stephen M. Gardiner wrote "A Perfect Moral Storm. The Ethical Tragedy of Climate Change, Oxford, Oxford UP", 2011.

Notes

1. "After years of recycling, carbon offsetting, and light bulbs changing, it is so obvious that individual action will never be an adequate response to climate change." From "On Fire" book by Naomi Klein, 2019.

2. "Governments have a stronger moral mandate than individuals to make things better. It is one of their principal duties to make things better for their own citizens, and they should cooperate to make things better for everyone." From "Climate Matters, Ethics in a Warming World" book by John Broome, 2012.

3. "Private morality of climate change also raises questions about how we should act in our private lives. Many of us have already taken some steps to reduce our emissions of greenhouse gas." From "Climate Matters, Ethics in a Warming World" book by John Broome, 2012.

4. "BP hired the public relations professionals Ogilvy & Mather to promote the slant that climate change is not the fault of an oil giant, but that of individuals." From "Big oil coined 'carbon footprints' to blame us for their greed. Keep them on the hook" by Rebecca Solnit in The Guardian, 2021.

5. The commercial begins with images of melting glaciers and the narrator explains "The Arctic ice is shrinking at a record pace [...] Electricity used by lighting is one of the biggest sources of CO2 emissions". The statement was false and it doesn't mention renewable energy, and what consumes electricity. Chevron also pointed at the replacement of light bulbs in commercials during the same years.

6. In Vandana Shiva's terms the "North exists in the South" by imposing global warming on the South (represented by countries in the global South and so-called third world) through higher per capita emissions. This asymmetrical globalization works for both causes and effects of climate change.

7. The book "The Travels of the T-Shirt in the Global Economy" by Pietra Rivoli, illustrates the character of much of the modern production, shipping, and marketing of common goods.

8. "How to Blow Up a Pipeline: Learning to Fight in a World on Fire" book by Andreas Malm, 2021.

9. "How to combat images that work toward assuring us of the controllability of climate change, even while they reinforce the idea that we are all responsible [...] which suggests – falsely – that we are all agents of climate change, sharing equally in its causes and effects." From "Against the Anthropocene: Visual Culture and Environment Today" book by TJ Demos, 2017.

SOCIO-SCIENTIFIC CONTEXT

Socio-Scientific Context

It's true that the climate fluctuates over centuries. This is how global warming is often compared with former climate anomalies such as the 'Little Ice Age' in Europe, and the 'Dust Bowl' drought in the United States, or to explain why the Sahara desert was once green. However, atmospheric concentrations of carbon dioxide, methane, and other gasses have increased to levels unprecedented in at least the last 800,000 years, which was long before humans first existed[1]. Comparing previous climate anomalies doesn't justify current epochal changes in the global climate system, and is misleading. We might know something about previous geological eras, measured in millions of years, however we don't know anything about how humans can continue to exist in an environment that has changed dramatically in only a century. These changes are ubiquitous globally[2], even if some geographical and urban areas are less affected than others. The consequences are greater than expected, and trigger chain reactions across countries, societies, and ecosystems[3]. The irreversibility of these changes is not always addressed. Although balance may be restored after a very long time, effects such as species extinction and the consequences on ecosystems are irreversible. Climate change can't be justified by finding quick solutions. Greenhouse gasses stay in the atmosphere for many hundreds, even thousands of years. They are going to affect the climate for centuries, and there is no solution to remove them. Also, carbon sinks, such as oceans, are at capacity. Forests that could absorb a portion of emissions take centuries to grow, and artificial carbon capture is inefficient. It's an irreversible situation, and even if global society enacts enough energy regulations to halt emissions and initiates energy transition measures, greenhouse gasses won't vanish and continue to accumulate in the present days.

This is probably not an apocalypse, humans won't become extinct, and nature won't end. Life on earth will reshape, migrate, and mutate. However, climate change does mean wars, diasporas, pandemics, and famines that will last for more than a century. It will affect humans for generations, bringing sorrow, trauma, deaths, and suffering. Something humans already experienced, often in the same fashion, first ignoring the damage until the destruction affects the lives of millions of innocent people. In the aftermath society will eventually recognize, monumentalize, reconcile, and reconstruct, as it happened after other human tragedies resulting from injustice such as genocides, slavery, and colonialism. Nevertheless, humans are just a small part of the earth's history, which has its own life and destiny, and very little to do with our small, precarious, and vulnerable existence. Other species experienced five mass extinctions already, and even the current sixth mass extinction[4] might regenerate a rebirth of genes adapted to new geological eras. Therefore, human cultural development should be the focus, rather than ice melting and forming, geological movements and layers, or species being extinguished every few dozens of million years.

Climate change is not about the earth's climate, it is instead about injustice and the consequential ethics that could help reshape our notion of justice. It is about human conscience in understanding the level of destruction and our felt sense of responsibility. This is a new "Age of Enlightenment" for humans, the only species able to produce and measure in detail such planetary change, and be able to articulate it with such sophisticated means. This intellectual awakening of being conscious of such conditions expands ethical justice from focusing solely on humans to ecosystems, other species, and the whole planet. From this unique moment for humans, a new ethics can emerge, a new humanism, and a new civilization. A global conscience that didn't exist before can already be seen in teenagers, as they unite around the world to create social movements, which weave together politics and economics of the whole planet for global justice[5]. This new anthropology is more interesting than a supposed new geology, and it might bring more than mere technical knowledge, traditional forms of governance, and economic development.

On the other hand, climate change is the ultimate "tragedy of the commons"[6] over which humans will inevitably escalate conflicts, creating authoritarian regimes, and economic inequalities never seen before[7]. We are already experiencing this new phase with the weaponization of the energy trade, the instrumentalization of climate disasters, and the rising of a "fossil fascism"[8]. Climate change has long been misrepresented as merely a scientific phenomenon, when in fact it is already a political instrument of power and a social catastrophe.

Notes

1. The first modern humans began migrating from Africa starting about 70,000-100,000 years ago. It has been estimated that 2023 has been the hottest in 100,000 years, and it will still continue to get hotter than it has been in hundreds of thousands of years.

2. In his book "The End of Nature" from 1989, Bill McKibben argues that what sets the contemporary world apart from any previous period of human history is, precisely, the capacity humans have for influencing their environment at a global level: Global warming, he says, is exactly that – global. We have now altered "every inch and every hour of the globe."

3. "The Sixth Extinction: An Unnatural History" book by Elizabeth Kolbert, 2014.

4. In May 2019, the Intergovernmental Science-Policy Platform on Biodiversity and Ecosystem Services published a report on the startling loss of wildlife around the world, warning that a million species of animals and plants are at risk of extinction.

5. On 20 September 2019: 16-year-old Greta Thunberg led the biggest climate protest in history, as around six million people across 150 countries joined together to demand greater action against climate change. And on 15 March 2019, 1.6 million students from 125 countries and more than 2,000 cities marched to demand urgent and decisive action against the climate crisis. The youth strikes for climate began with a solo protest by Greta Thunberg in Sweden in August 2018.

6. The tragedy of the commons is a metaphoric label for a concept that is widely discussed in economics, ecology, and other sciences. The metaphor is the title of a 1968 essay by ecologist Garrett Hardin. As example, he cited a watercourse which all are free to pollute. But the principal concern of his essay was overpopulation of the planet.

7. "The convergence of growing economic inequality, social, and political corruption, corporate oligarchy, police brutality, the criminalization of protest and civil disobedience, and the destruction of the environment" by TJ Demos from "Against the Anthropocene: Visual Culture and Environment Today", 2017.

8. "White Skin, Black Fuel: On the Danger of Fossil Fascism" book by Andreas Malm and the Zetkin Collective, 2021.

Cultural Context

Knowledge and culture around climate change have largely been influenced by the fossil fuel industry. Literacy, language, and semiotics have been used for deception and censorship. The fossil fuel industry managed to mislead journalists, researchers, artists, intellectuals, politicians, and eventually all of society by spreading misinformation, keeping studies secret, and not being mentioned in debates and policies. As a result there have been several misconceptions, misunderstandings, and misrepresentations of climate change's political and economic causes and effects. Climate change is about media ecology, cultural politics, and the knowledge economy, specifically how they have been compromised. The cultural influence of the fossil fuels industry is vast and subtle, operating both in secret through covert operations, and in public to gain social legitimacy. This influence on culture and knowledge delays and weakens the tackling of global warming, and thus is a major force driving the climate crisis as much as economic and political factors.

Literacy

In most of the literature, philosophy, and art about climate change there is often an epistemic gap due to an ontological mistake, which is to not include the study of the fossil fuel industry and its historic role. The industry's soft power obfuscated knowledge in scientific and intellectual research. For decades they had major economic influence inside universities, cultural institutions, and mainstream media to avoid public, political, scientific, and intellectual discourse around them. Even the most quoted philosophers in this field barely mention the word "fossil fuel" (see most of the writing of Bruno Latour[1]), and the majority of political debates make no reference to the power of these companies. Art and science museums didn't discussed their role because fossil fuel firms were often their main donors, and the media didn't report on them because they were often their major sponsors.

Fossil fuel companies have interfered in literacy on climate change directly from the inside of universities where researchers, professors, and students studied the phenomena. For decades most of the courses on climate change at universities didn't mention the interests of the producers of fossil fuels. Most international universities such as Stanford, MIT, Harvard, and NYU accepted large donations from fossil fuel companies, who could even decide the funding of scientists and research programs[2]. These donations were not only to control the institutions, but also to manipulate scientific findings, which is what happened at the Smithsonian Institution for instance, one of America's oldest and most respected scientific research organizations[3]. Campaigns to block the fossil fuel industry's influence inside universities are ongoing around the world, but meanwhile students and researchers are still being misled. Fossil fuel firms also steered the teaching of climate change in high schools and even in kindergartens, as they recognized that new generations might turn against the use of fossil fuels[4].

As a result, the actual causes of climate change were hidden, fossil fuel private interests were erased, and they were always given less consideration in intellectual argumentations. Unfortunately, climate change has been mostly described as a scientific problem. In the first decades of popularizing the phenomenon, the cause was explained through the 'greenhouse effect' with visuals, media features, books, and papers. However, there was no mention of who benefited from producing products that generate greenhouse gasses. Later the literacy around climate change started to focus on 'anthropogenic' causes, the idea that human activities were to blame, but never too specifically about which activities and which humans. Then the 'anthropogenic' causes would focus on animal farming, agriculture, or deforestation, but still no mention of the producers of the fuel that drives all those activities, which indeed contribute to emissions, but are not the main sources.

It hasn't only been misinformation spread by fossil fuel companies and the green-washing of the business world that led to the dismissal of global warming. Still today, the same institutions that claim to be at the forefront of climate advocacy don't even mention the global fossil fuel economy. Universities, cultural institutions, the art world, and the media increasingly run special programs about climate change, but without examining its cause, the fossil fuel industry, which often even funds such institutions.

Linguistics

By influencing the understanding and perception of climate change, linguistics plays a significant role in creating deception and misconceptions. Even the term 'climate change' itself is instrumentalized. Historically, this manipulation dates back to the 2004 campaign led by conservative communication strategist Frank Luntz, who believed the term 'global warming' evoked greater concern, while 'climate change' sounded less alarming.

This politics of linguistics is still present today with conservative opinion leaders, politicians, and journalists referring to global warming by using other subtle terminology and language. On the other hand, activists prefer terms such as 'climate crisis' or 'climate emergency' to emphasize its urgency and gravity. After all, the same notion of 'change' may no longer be explicative as the climate breakdown accelerates and is normalized, as well as for the ideas of 'crisis' and 'emergency'. For instance, for a long time cultural production about climate change focused on raising awareness, while recently the focus is on documenting and engaging with the losses.

The instrumental use of linguistics extends to today's language around solutions for climate change, with terms such as sustainability, offsetting, footprint, renewables, decarbonization, and netzero, which are used to comfort public concerns rather than being effective solutions. Often these terms are used out of context, as keywords that serve as branding or ideological positioning, while the real culprits, economies, politics, and history remain disguised.

As a result, the language surrounding climate change is now largely codified with terminologies and linguistic formulas that often contribute to ethics-washing and green-washing, which today often replace the disinformation and misinformation around climate change.

Semiotics

Climate change is a complex semiotic system. The multiple signs and significations of climate change are often orchestrated to manipulate meaning. The always more present signs of climate breakdown are stripped from their referents. For instance, even if they signify destruction resulting from climate change, they don't produce meanings to generate logical consequential reactions. The signification produced by the semiotic machine of the fossil fuel industry is able to nullify meanings, removing them from concrete reality despite evident signs of direct harm.

Semiotically, climate change is being disguised by constructing a discrepancy between the subject and its representation. Even though science has been pinpointing for a long time how fossil fuels are the cause of climate change, the meaning of this science lacks a concrete referent, which is the industry that produces fossil fuels. This semiotic mismatch has resulted in misrepresentation and misunderstanding, generating confusion that lingers in the cultural world and in society. In today's new era of denialism, it is not the climate emergency that is being denied, but rather the causes and the culprits that are mystified. Today green-washing and green-politics is based on a semiotic mismatch between facts and action, as well as rhetoric and reality, which creates even more confusion and detachment from the subject of climate change.

Nevertheless, human subjectivity naturally responds to signs of climate collapse and disasters, which often results in a prevailing sense of fear, anxiety, depression, hopelessness, grief, and melancholy. The current threat produces eschatological meanings from which humans need to escape to survive. The challenge of the semiotics of climate change is not only how we decipher the signs, but also how we take control of meanings to contrast future normalizations of disasters and what causes them[5]. However, the semiology of climate change needs to take into consideration social bubbles, as people live in completely different realities, polarized by social media algorithms and sharp socioeconomic inequalities, which create very different significations and meanings.

Deception

For decades major fossil fuel companies have worked to distort climate science findings, deceive the public, and block policies designed to hasten a needed transition to a clean energy economy. Alongside spreading misinformation through education, culture, and media, fossil fuel companies also engaged in political collusion through front groups and secret funding to hide their influence and avoid accountability. Even if fossil fuel company leaders knew about the consequences of their products, they developed or participated in campaigns to deliberately deceive the public, deny the harm, and block policies designed to reduce greenhouse emissions[6]. The campaign of deception continues today, employing increasingly subtle strategies by various groups using plans that align with the agendas of fossil fuel companies. Presently, they operate through proxies, utilizing predominantly ideological groups, such as political conservative organizations, or through commercial operations, which involve purchasing stakes in large businesses or providing sponsorships. They persist in influencing the general public through means such as controlling entire media outlets, or even entire media platforms, as well as through content creation and influencers.

In today's social media landscape, there is a surge of renewed climate change denial, focusing on false solutions or denying they are needed. This new denial is often about political attacks on those who advocate for regulations, renewable energy, de-growth, and accountability. Social media has had a major role in polarizing society on climate change, which can be traced historically. Until the late 1990s climate change was a bipartisan issue, for instance, U.S. Republicans had a leading role in addressing it[7]. Even if measures have been adapted to curb misinformation about climate change on social media, there is a new explosion of malicious content and manipulation. This trend is particularly evident on platforms like Twitter, where Elon Musk took control in 2022. The platform's algorithms tend to promote climate change denial content, while bots aggressively target climate advocacy. Also on YouTube, a recent research[8] found an increase of 35% in the past 6 years of all climate denial claims in popular videos.

Secrecy

The secrecy around climate change pertains to a large body of evidence on the criminal behavior of the fossil fuel industry. Beginning with the amount of emissions that each company produces[9] based on their extraction and trade of fossil fuels, which was revealed only through the effort of independent researchers using the carbon majors' data[10]. Amongst the data on their production, there were also studies on how their products cause climate change, which for decades they kept secret, before they were finally revealed by investigative journalists[11]. Secrecy is maintained through corporate power in the form of confidential memos, non-disclosure agreements, and trade secrets contracts. It's fair to imagine that several corporate studies and plans concerning the future that climate change will bring, are still being kept secret. Secrecy is especially subtle regarding the funding of lobbies and campaigns to deceive policy makers and the public. The so-called 'dark money' groups do not reveal their funders, and are known to have supported contrarian scientific research in several institutions[12]. Fossil fuels firms' financial secrecy concerns also economic agreements, contractual vehicles, licenses for drilling and mining, commercial agreements, and offshore transactions, capitals, and entities. They can use these vehicles to corrupt governments and blackmail politicians. For instance, the bargaining of licenses to extract new gas and oil, or build pipelines is shrouded in secrecy, with negotiations taking place behind closed doors. Profits accumulated are often sheltered in tax havens around the world where financial secrecy protects them from scrutiny, tariffs, and sanctions. They even have special instruments also for legal disputes, like in the case of the Energy Charter Treaty (ECT), which is a court system that operates in secrecy[13] to protect the interests of the fossil fuel industry.

Moreover, the very history of how and what really produced climate change remained concealed for a long time, not providing material for reflection and action. Even though climate change has been a widely known issue since the 1980s and 1990s, it was in the 2010s that data and documents on the sources and studies were unveiled, and only in the 2020s a broader conversation started to focus on ending fossil fuel and looking at specific responsibilities.

Invisibility

Climate change has certain built-in invisibilities[14]. Aside from scientists, the empirical knowledge around climate change has at last become visible after decades. It's this cultural context that could enable the manufacturing of misconception and denial, as self-evident evidence on the climate breakdown has only become more visible as of the 2020s, and thus the damage caused didn't garner public outrage like in the case of other forms of violence. This form of "slow violence"[15] contracts and expands with always more acceleration and intensification of destruction, which in turn will bring more social conflicts and inequalities.

The fact that greenhouse gasses are not visible to humans has defined carbon dioxide (CO_2) as an "invisible pollutant", and other gasses are even less visible. For instance cameras and satellites to monitor methane have been available only in the past few years. These new cameras provided new evidence on the leaks that the fossil fuels industry failed to address for decades. Methane (CH_4) is the second largest contributor to global warming and it is 86 times more potent than CO_2. Even if it remains in the atmosphere for only a couple of decades, cutting methane pollution from the oil and gas industry is the fastest way to slow climate change, however the industry has avoided addressing this[16]. Another lesser known greenhouse gas is sulfur hexafluoride (SF_6), with a single pound of SF_6 polluting 25,000 times more than CO_2 and remaining in the atmosphere for 3,200 years. However, the EPA and UN do not regulate the emissions of these potent greenhouse gasses, and leaks by the energy industry are rarely reported[17] and therefore invisible to citizens.

In addition to the invisibility of atmospheric balance[18], climate change runs deeply through invisible microorganisms and microecosystems, which in turn are connected to larger ecosystems. Organisms ranging from bacteria to insects, trigger chain reactions that impact the food supply for several species including humans. These effects are more visible to vulnerable populations, often in remote areas of the world, while they remain invisible to the ones that live in urban environments where adaptation to climate change is possible.

This invisibility also concerns the opacity created by climate change denialists, particularly individuals and corporations directly linked to the fossil fuel industry that have deliberately obfuscated irrefutable evidence[19]. These regimes of visibilities affect the formation of knowledge and culture, which are still lacking in the media, arts, and education systems. Cultural producers should disrupt these invisibilities and elaborate new forms of visibility in order to inform, create awareness, and mobilize their audiences.

Notes

1. Alongside not mentioning the role of fossil fuels, Bruno Latour was already criticized in "The Shock of the Anthropocene", 2016. Christophe Bonneuil and Jean-Baptiste Fressoz lamented the inability of preeminent philosophies of science to theorize the event of climate change. They found Bruno Latour especially culpable, charging him with having bought into the myth of a "great divide" between nature and society.

2. "The fossil fuel industry's invisible colonization of academia". Article by Ben Franta from The Guardian, 2017.

3. The documents, obtained through a FOIA request by Greenpeace and the Climate Investigations Center, show that scientist Wei-Hock Soon received millions in research funding from fossil fuel interests including ExxonMobil, the American Petroleum Institute (API), the Charles Koch Foundation, and Southern Company, a large electric utility in Atlanta that generates most of its power from coal.

4. In the year 2000, the American Legislative Exchange Council (ALEC) launched the "Environmental Literacy Improvement Act" to legislate the teaching of climate science denial as school curricula. ALEC donors included General Motors, BP America, Chevron, ExxonMobil and Shell, and electric utility companies Duke Energy, Entergy, and Progress Energy. In 1998, a section of the American Petroleum Institute (API) roadmap memo of the Global Climate Science Communications Team outlined a plan to target the National Science Teachers Association. In October 2002, it was once again the API who carried out the plan to distribute curriculum materials that question established science through the National Science Teachers Association by running the website Classroom Energy!, which offers lesson plans and materials for teachers from kindergarten through high school.

5. "'Normalization' is not merely the process of humans adapting to a situation after the disaster; it is much more an ideological process through which the very abnormality of a given situation is being transformed into something that is now described as the 'new normal'." From "After the Apocalypse" book by Srećko Horvat, Polity, 2021.

6. For instance the American Petroleum Institute (API) deception continues to this day in other forms – outlining plans to reach the media, the public, and policy makers with a message emphasizing uncertainties in climate science.

7. George H.W. Bush had a reputation as a moderate conservative Republican. When he ran for office, he said that he was going to address the problem of climate change, and he specifically said he was going to bring the power of the 'White House effect' to fight the greenhouse effect.

8. In a report called "New Denial" published in 2024, the Centre for Countering Digital Hate evaluated the content of over 12,000 YouTube videos from 96 channels.

9. "Oil firms should disclose carbon output" article from The Guardian, 2021.

10. In 2013, Rick Heede, co-founder and director of the Climate Accountability Institute, authors a peer-reviewed study revealing that 90 producers of oil, natural gas, coal, and cement – the 'Carbon Majors' – are responsible for 63 percent of cumulative industrial carbon dioxide and methane emissions worldwide between 1751 and 2010. Just 28 companies have been responsible for 25 percent of all emissions since 1965.

11. The first journalistic investigation on Exxon secret research and knowledge on climate change was published in late 2015 by InsideClimate News and the Los Angeles Times, in collaboration with Columbia University's School of Journalism.

12. For instance, according to one in-depth study, Donors Trust – which has received millions of dollars from Koch foundations – distributed dozens of millions to groups – including the Heartland Institute, Americans for Prosperity, and the Committee for a Constructive Tomorrow – that deny the science and impacts of human-caused climate change and the need to cut global warming emissions.

13. "The European Commission aims to end the secret system protecting fossil fuel holdings" article from the Guardian, 2021.

14. "Climate change is often invisible, or rather invisibilized, so as to reinforce its apparent separateness from social and political realms". From "The Routledge Companion to Contemporary Art, Visual Culture, and Climate Change" edited by T. J. Demos, Emily Eliza Scott, and Subhankar Banerjee, 2021.

15. As scholar Rob Nixon argues, many environmental problems amount to a form of 'slow violence'. As he states: "Stories of toxic build-up, massing greenhouse gasses, and accelerated species loss due to ravaged habitats are all cataclysmic, but they are scientific convoluted cataclysms in which casualties are postponed, often for generations."

16. "Methane emissions from oil and gas are worse than reported to the UN, satellites show" and "Leaks of potent greenhouse gas could be easily fixed, say experts, and would rapidly reduce global heating" article from the Guardian, 2023.

17. In 2020, Duke Energy, which provides electricity in six U.S. states, leaked nearly 11 metric tons of SF6 into the atmosphere from its electric substations in North and South Carolina alone; these emissions were equal to the annual greenhouse gas emissions of more than 59,000 automobiles.

18. "Visualization ranges from the translation of research outcomes into visual output and broadly encompasses experimental, hybrid, and cross-cutting cultural practices. To visualize atmospheric politics first requires critically framing visuality itself" by Amy Balkin from the essay "Visualizing Atmospheric Politics", 2021.

19. "Corporate polluters use sophisticated strategies to make their pollution, emission, and responsibility invisible. The production of invisibility is concerted and formidable. What artistic strategies might disrupt this gigantic manufacture of opacity?" by Oliver Ressler from the book "Barricading the Ice Sheets", 2020.

POLITICAL ECONOMIC
CONTEXT

Political Economic Context

The political economic context of climate change needs to take in account the reality of the economy of fossil fuels and its global politics. The concepts of the 'Green New Deal' and 'Energy Transition' are increasingly presented as political and economic promises by governments and corporations, yet the reality remains concealed. Data on fossil fuel production and consumption is often not disclosed, and there is no transparency on the several political interests to protect the industry.

The Economic Context

The Industrial Revolution marked the beginning of mass use of fossil fuels, however, it was only with rapid globalization that the rate of greenhouse emissions sped up dramatically. It's since 1988 that more than half of all industrial carbon emissions have been released into the atmosphere. This when major fossil fuel companies and governments indisputably knew the consequences of expanding such an economy. International trade with new markets in China and Russia resulted in the accelerated use of fossil fuels[1], yet the United States remains the biggest oil producer in the world. From the 1980s to today, oil production in the United States has skyrocketed, going from around eight million barrels per day in 1983, to over thirteen million barrels per day in 2023. A leap made possible above all by the exploitation in the last decade of reserves of so-called shale oil and shale gas, trapped among rocks and extracted with the 'fracking' technique. This new form of extraction has contributed to an extraordinary increase not only in CO2, but also leaks of methane, which is a much more powerful greenhouse gas than carbon dioxide. Aside from oil, the U.S. is also the biggest producer of natural gas with a new production record in 2023. China and India are instead left with being the biggest producers of coal, which does generate more CO2 than crude oil, but the amount of extraction and trade is smaller. The U.S. should undergo deeper scrutiny for its historical and current role in benefitting from crude oil. The sale of fossil fuel can be very lucrative, as the production is controlled by the very few countries that own the technology to produce it, and have the power to control extraction sites. Renewable energy is in turn more accessible and less expensive to produce, which means it is less lucrative, and this is why fossil fuels producers are not embracing it. As a result, only 5% of total energy is made from renewable sources such as wind and solar.

The production of fossil fuels concerns also its consumption, calculated per capita, in reference to the average consumption by each person in a particular population. The U.S. is the greatest consumer of crude oil, beyond an astonishing 900 of yearly gallons per capita, compared to the second largest consumer, China, with 140 of yearly gallons per capita, meaning that Americans consume oil at a rate approximately 10 times higher than the global average. The consumption of fossil fuels can be measured in the amount of flights, cars, goods, and everything that is consumed in large quantities. Promoting and defending such consumption is key for the producers. Naturally, industries and countries with vested interests in increasing consumption and fostering addiction to fossil fuels are often the very ones responsible for their production. However, dependence on the fossil fuel economy runs deeper than it seems. In the United States, for example, a significant portion of pension funds are invested in the stocks of profitable fossil fuel companies. Even in countries where these companies are nationalized, the revenues generated from the sales play a fundamental role in providing essential social welfare services.

Paradoxically, the consumption of fossil fuels is also bolstered by public subsidies[2]. For instance, subsidies from governments that cut the price of fuels for consumers doubled in 2022, with a record $7 trillion as governments supported consumers and businesses during the global spike in energy prices caused by Russia's invasion of Ukraine, and the economic recovery from the pandemic. However these subsidies benefit mostly the fossil fuel industry, while consumers pay the consequences with fewer subsidies for renewable energy and funds for climate disasters.

Governments do take into consideration the social cost of fossil fuels, known as the "Social Cost of Carbon" (SCC). This economic concept represents the estimated monetary value of the net societal harms associated with the release of one metric ton of carbon dioxide (CO_2) into the atmosphere. The SCC encompasses not only current damages from CO_2 emissions, but also the long-term impact on future generations. However, it's worth noting that the SCC value varies from one government to another, often appearing somewhat arbitrary. In the United States, during the Obama administration, the federal SCC was estimated to be approximately $50 per metric ton, a value that the Biden administration has maintained. Nonetheless, some studies suggest a significantly higher estimate, around $185 per metric ton of carbon dioxide emitted. Importantly, even this higher value doesn't fully account for the economic inequality and the harm experienced by individuals, nor does it address the economic consequences resulting from the potential collapse of critical infrastructures.

These costs should ideally be covered through the implementation of a carbon tax, which historically has not been applied to fossil fuel companies as they have opposed it for decades through lobbying efforts and manipulation of public opinion. Instead, many countries have imposed national carbon taxes on consumption, shifting the burden onto workers and everyday citizens, who end up shouldering the cost of the damages they will still inevitably suffer. While taxes on consumers increase the cost of living, fossil fuel industries often enjoy various privileges, including subsidies, tax breaks, and royalty-free offshore profits. Currently, carbon taxes vary widely from one country to another, with each nation adopting individual tax rates and scopes. In some cases, carbon taxes are either absent or unbalanced between social classes of consumers. Ideally, the revenue generated from a carbon tax should be reinvested directly and transparently in renewable energy sources. Unfortunately, in many instances, these revenues are diverted towards fossil fuel subsidies, a consequence that defies logic.

In the financialization of climate change, there are several nonsense economic vehicles that delay genuine and effective solutions. The so called Net-Zero, Carbon Neutral, and EU Emissions Trading System (ETS) of Carbon Credits are instances of complex accounting and trading schemes to keep burning fossil fuels, and eventually to make it even more profitable with the help of these financial vehicles[3]. For instance, the current value of the Carbon Credits trade is substantial and continues to grow with several countries joining. As of 2022, the global Carbon Credits market was valued at approximately $2 billion and projections suggest a significant increase, with the trade expected to reach around $143.5 billion by 2032. Although this market is in expansion, the value of the Carbon Credit is extremely volatile, and the uneven performance of this financial commodity has already resulted in several crashes that left many companies bankrupt. Moreover, a number of scandals already revealed how Carbon Credits are not only ineffective in halting emissions, but may even increase them. At this time, there hasn't been admission of failure by the United Nations, EU, or G8 nations that introduced the scheme. Carbon Credits are valued based on each metric ton of CO_2. The most common equivalency for pricing Carbon Credits is based on Global Warming Potential (GWP), in which GWP does not account for the difference in time that each greenhouse gas remains in the atmosphere. Also the Social Cost of climate change doesn't account for the price of Carbon Credits. Ultimately, the price of Carbon Credits in markets can range from a few dollars to over $20 per ton. These values fluctuate and can be inflated, making it a nonsense billion-dollar speculative financial market.

Meanwhile, profits for major fossil fuel companies increased significantly in the aftermath of Russia's invasion of Ukraine. Some of the largest oil and gas firms reported record profits for the year 2022, which were attributed to the high prices of energy during this period. For example, BP reported net profits of $27.7 billion for 2022, Shell also reported almost $40 billion in profit, meaning both firms doubled their profits from 2021. In the United States, ExxonMobil posted a record $56 billion profit for 2022, a 143.48% increase from 2021. Saudi Arabia company Aramco's net income increased by 46.5% to a record $161.1 billion in 2022, compared to $110.0 billion in 2021.

The Political Context

The politics of climate change can be seen only as an international effort to limit extraction and use of fossil fuel. Something that has not resulted in significant reductions, and the truth is that the largest fossil fuel extraction projects to date have only begun in recent years. Referred to as 'Carbon Bombs'[4], these new major fossil fuels projects are permitted and supported by the same governments that call for climate change regulations. Moreover, in international negotiation venues, like in the Conference of the Parties (COP), the power and interests of the fossil fuel industry is not addressed[5]. Even in the 2015 Paris Climate Agreement there is no mention of the words 'fossil fuels', 'coal', 'oil', or 'gas' once.

The political lobby of the fossil fuel industry can operate through direct bribery or subtle influence with trade associations, think tanks, and revolving-doors. For instance in the United States the American Legislative Exchange Council (ALEC) provides a venue for industry groups to influence policy makers behind closed doors. Leaked internal documents show that ALEC, backed by many major fossil fuel companies such as Chevron, ExxonMobil, Peabody Energy, and Shell, continue to serve as an important conduit for climate misinformation and policy proposals designed to block climate action until very recently. Much of ALEC's lobbying has focused on dismantling policies that have proven effective in reducing carbon pollution and accelerating the transition to clean energy.

The political influence of fossil fuels is often subtler, as they achieve social legitimation by sponsoring culture, sport, and media. Or it can be more direct with payments to politicians as forms of bribery; for instance, countries like Saudi Arabia, Qatar, Abu Dhabi, and Oman allegedly secretly paid several millions of dollars to political leaders and opinion makers such as Nicolas Sarkozy and Bernard-Henry Levy in France, Thabo Mbeki in South Africa, even Benjamin Netanyahu in Israel. Saudi Arabian government funds have been paid out to a former prime minister in Italy, Matteo Renzi, in a legal and rather transparent way. The recent so-called 'Qatargate' in European Parliament was just the tip of the iceberg. In the United Kingdom, Abu Dhabi is buying major media outlets like the Telegraph and the Spectator, aiming to influence public opinion and therefore the British parliament, even hiring a government party insider, former minister Osborne. A Riyadh sovereign fund has poured two billion dollars into the private equity vehicle of Jared Kushner, Donald Trump's son-in-law, who in turn was the candidate favored by polls for the White House[6]. Fossil fuels companies have also the major interest in controlling politics for securing permits and licenses on drilling and mining for extracting and transporting fossil fuels at sites within various sovereign territories[7]. The construction of transnational pipelines, offshore platforms, and extensive mining involves exceptional political negotiations, frequently conducted behind closed doors, including agreements made through bribes and the exchange of significant political favors.

Indeed the politics of climate change is about the global economy. Currently, there are no real international tariffs or embargoes policies on countries considered large producers of fossil fuels. International trade agreements such as the General Agreement on Tariffs and Trade (GATT) of the World Trade Organization (WTO) do allow members to maintain measures that are "necessary to protect human, animal or plant life or health", but only as long as they are "not applied in a manner which would constitute a means of arbitrary or unjustifiable discrimination between countries where the same conditions prevail, or a disguised restriction on international trade". These supposed discriminations make the implementation of carbon tariffs, also known as border carbon adjustments (BCAs), a complex political challenge, and can lead to deadlocks in international negotiations.

Fossil fuels production is part of bigger political contexts, which only geopolitics can explain, and only international institutions can govern. Some of these global politics of fossil fuels are explained in the following pages.

Notes

1. The international trade allowed these countries to move their dirty production to places like China or India. The rise in emissions from goods produced in developing countries but consumed in industrialized ones is six times greater than the emission savings of industrialized countries.

2. The amount of subsidies dedicated to developing renewable energy is very little compared to subsidies for fossil fuel. For instance, fossil fuels received £20bn more UK support than renewables since 2015, which equal to 0.01% of subsidies in the energy sector. One-fifth of money was given directly to the fossil fuel industry to support new extraction and mining. These percentages are to this day similar in many other countries.

3. "Ending Fossil Fuels. Why Net Zero is Not Enough" book by Holly Jean Buck, Verso, 2021.

4. "Revealed: the 'carbon bombs' set to trigger catastrophic climate breakdown". Dossier from The Guardian, 2022.

5. Only in 2012, for the first time, the term "Fossil Fuels" was mentioned during UN climate negotiations. Only in 2019 it was first mentioned at the COP. In 2023 and 2024 the presidents of the COP were fossil fuel company executives and before the industry lobbyists had unfettered access to interfere in the negotiation process.

6. In January 2019, Reuters uncovered information about Project Raven. Among other things, it uncovered the extent of the Qatari system of payments to politicians and influential public figures from different countries.

7. Some noticeable scandals of bribery and corruption: The Nigerian Oil Scandal (1970s), UN Oil-for-Food Scandal (1995-2003), Halliburton Bribery Scandal (2000); Brazil's Petrobras Scandal (2014), and several others.

Geopolitical Context

A common misconception about climate change politics is the belief that state regulations, global treaties, and agreements can resolve conflicts among countries competing for control over fossil fuel reserves and trade, which is inevitably connected to military and economic power. One perspective is that climate change is not solely a byproduct of capitalism, but rather a result of imperialist agendas or national security concerns, as fossil fuel firms frequently argue in U.S. courts.

Understanding the politics of the Petrodollar is crucial for navigating the geopolitical landscape of the fossil fuel industry in the last century. After the first decades of the Industrial Revolution, which was marked by the use of coal as the main source of energy, oil began to replace it with the advent of combustion engine technology, and the production of plastics and chemical compounds derived from oil. These developments led to an increasing demand for oil, and at this point the United States still maintained dominance, with enough reserves and leading technology to extract it.

Due to the dominance of Anglo-American powers in the oil economy, the Organization of Petroleum Exporting Countries (OPEC) was established in 1961. Initially, it consisted of Saudi Arabia, Iraq, Kuwait, Iran, and Venezuela for safeguarding the sovereignty of each country's natural resources. Over time, additional members joined, including Algeria, Angola, the Republic of the Congo, Equatorial Guinea, Gabon, Libya, Nigeria, and the United Arab Emirates. In 1971, during the United States' increasing demand for oil and declining domestic production, President Nixon imposed price ceilings on oil. This move led to a greater reliance on foreign oil imports, as low prices encouraged higher consumption.

In 1973, the Western world faced the Oil Crisis as Arab OPEC members imposed an embargo on the United States. This crisis prompted the creation of the Petrodollar system through a deal between the U.S. and Saudi Arabia. The agreement involved pricing and trading oil exclusively in U.S. dollars. The pact was struck following the 1973 Arab-Israeli War, as Arab OPEC nations retaliated against the U.S. for supplying the Israeli military, and aimed to gain leverage in post-war peace negotiations. The embargo was triggered by the Yom Kippur War in October 1973 when a coalition of Arab states, led by Egypt and Syria, launched a surprise attack on Israel during the holiest day on the Jewish calendar. Subsequently, in 1975, Saudi Arabia and the U.S. signed military contracts worth approximately $2 billion, ensuring the protection of oil fields through U.S. military power, while also ensuring that oil sales would exclusively be in U.S. dollars. By the end of 1975, all remaining OPEC nations had also agreed to price their oil in dollars.

Lately, there have been changes that Saudi Arabia has been making to drop the Petrodollar – particularly regarding them leaning towards the Chinese Yuan. China and Russia, agreed to make settlements in currencies other than the U.S. dollar, already in 2022 with the beginning of the war in Ukraine. In February 2022 alone, China imported over 2 million barrels of Russian crude, a new record high. Other major OPEC nations and BRICS members (Brazil, Russia, India, and South Africa) are either accepting the Yuan already or strongly considering it. Russia, Iran, and Venezuela account for about 40% of the world's official oil fields, and the three sell their oil in exchange for the Yuan. Turkey, Argentina, Indonesia and heavyweight oil producer Saudi Arabia have all applied for admittance into BRICS.

These recent developments show that as long as the global economy is dependent on fossil fuels, petro-dictators can influence global energy prices as a weapon. While the U.S. is drilling more oil than ever, globally the amount of barrels of crude oil is increasing, as well as the production of methane. Climate change concerns the political dominance of the global market of fossil fuels, rather than local policies to limit greenhouse emissions.

Global political institutions

The global political institutions that address climate change are often influenced by the interests of the fossil fuel industry. Even when some of these political institutions operate independently and hold sincere intentions, they often lack the enforcement power necessary to implement policy proposals promptly and effectively, resulting in delays that can span several decades. The following glossary of international institutions underscores their failure in effectively addressing climate change.

UN, United Nations
Created the IPCC and the COP with a strong commitment to monitor and negotiate policies around climate change, however it has no power to enforce policies. Even the Paris Agreement can be withdrawn from, as the U.S. did during the Trump administration. The UN is not able to negotiate with the fossil fuels industry, which is even allowed to lobby at the COP, compromising any meaningful policy. Furthermore, the UN engages with false climate solutions such as Carbon Capture, and the failing system of Carbon Credits.

IMF, International Monetary Fund
Offers loans with high-interest rates to countries facing financial difficulties, which are often invested in fossil fuel extraction. These extracted fossil fuels are then often sold to western companies at a fraction of the market price, resulting in significant costs for the borrowing country and further exacerbating its debt with the IMF and other lenders.

World Bank
The major source of subsidies for fossil fuel projects, providing financial support to various aspects of the fossil fuel industry around the world. These subsidies to the fossil fuel industry are meant to reduce the cost of the energy and thus supposedly boost the economy, which meanwhile is impacted by climate disasters. The World Bank notoriously impoverished third-world countries with dramatic debt levels and it has been a major promoter of the

Carbon Credits system that has generated speculation and the destruction of ecosystems worldwide.

WTO, World Trade Organization

An international organization that deals with global trade rules and resolving trade disputes among member countries. Proposals for international carbon tax and tariffs are obstructed by trading countries, who threaten action through the WTO. Any trade taxation on greenhouse emissions would need to be consistent with the rules of WTO agreements, without which the pursuit of global carbon neutrality would ultimately be in vain.

GATT, General Agreement on Tariffs and Trade

A legal agreement between many countries, whose overall purpose was to promote international trade by reducing or eliminating trade barriers such as tariffs or quotas. It is now used as the main opposition to establish tariffs on the import and export of fossil fuels, and the products that derive from intensive use of fossil fuels.

OECD, Organization for Economic Co-operation and Development

An intergovernmental organization with 38 member countries to stimulate economic progress and world trade. Even if it is active in assessing the impact of climate change on the global economy, it lacks enforcement power and its recommendations are not taken into consideration.

OPEC, Organization of the Petroleum Exporting Countries

An organization of leading oil-producing countries in opposition to western countries in order to collectively influence the global oil market and maximize profit. It has the ability to manipulate the price of crude oil internationally, and has the veto of Saudi Arabia. Most of its members are authoritarian countries and together they control more than 40% of oil produced globally.

ECT, Energy Charter Treaty

An international agreement that establishes a multilateral framework for cross-border cooperation in the energy industry, principally the fossil fuel industry. It's considered a secret court that is used by the fossil fuel industry to block any prohibition to extract fossil fuel from licensed sites in foreign countries.

IEA, International Energy Agency

An autonomous intergovernmental organization that provides policy recommendations, analysis, and data on the entire global energy sector. It can provide data on the amount of greenhouse emissions from each fossil fuel company, however it can't enforce transparency to obtain accurate data.

EPA, U.S. Environmental Protection Agency

A federal agency responsible for protecting human health and the environment in the United States. It enacted the first air quality legislations, however it initially resisted classifying carbon dioxide (CO_2) as a pollutant under the Clean Air Act. Only in 2009, during the Obama administration, EPA formally declared that greenhouse gasses, including CO_2, posed a threat.

COP, UN Conference of the Parties

Brings together nations every year to assess and address global climate change issues, negotiate international climate agreements, and coordinate efforts to adapt to the effects of climate change. In 2023 and 2024 the presidents of COPs were fossil fuel executives and the number of lobbyists at COP increased from 504 to 2456 in the past two years. For decades the words 'fossil fuel' were not mentioned in any official climate negotiation at COPs, the first time was only in 2019.

IPCC, UN Intergovernmental Panel on Climate Change

Typically releases comprehensive assessment reports every 6-7 years. These reports provide updated and authoritative scientific information on climate change, its impact, and potential mitigation and adaptation strategies, helping to inform global climate policy and action. However, with accelerating climate collapse the IPCC reports are not updated frequently enough, so their forecasts lag behind.

UNFCCC, UN Framework Convention on Climate Change

Serves as the primary international treaty for addressing climate change. Its role is to facilitate global cooperation among nations to prevent climate change. This includes the negotiation of international agreements like the Kyoto Protocol and the Paris Agreement. However, the United States, Canada, and Australia did not ratify the Kyoto Protocol. After the Paris Agreement of 2015, there hasn't been significant new agreements and greenhouse emissions continue to increase.

POLITICAL AND ECONOMIC SOLUTIONS

What is really needed:

• Banning Investments, Production, and Extraction of Fossil Fuels.

• Banning Greenwashing, Sponsorships, and Disinformation by the Fossil Fuels industry.

• Taxing Profits, Pollution, Production, and Extraction of Fossil Fuels.

Others means to curb the Fossil Fuel industry: Embargoes, Sanctions, Expropriations, Fines, and Penalties.

The industry should convert into:

• Renewable energy.

• Fixing gas leaks.

• Cleaning extraction sites.

• Natural CO_2 removal.

CLIMATE LITIGATION

Climate Litigation

Climate litigation involves legal actions where individuals, organizations, or governments seek legal remedies to address climate change effects, or hold entities accountable for contributing to climate harm. A turning point of climate litigation occurred in the Netherlands on June 24, 2015, with a sentence in the Hague[1], which was immediately defined by experts as a historic ruling, because for the first time judicial power could be considered even more effective than legislative power in tackling climate change legally. The trial was against the state of the Netherlands for the reduction of emissions and similar to a victorious sentence against Shell in 2021[2]. There are several other climate lawsuits against governments and states for the reduction of emissions or violations of human rights, however, climate litigation here is intended to seek financial compensation for reparations, preservation, adaptation, and as a form of penalty.

Compensation claims from citizens, stakeholders, and internal shareholders against fossil fuel companies are based on the amount of greenhouse emissions generated by each fossil fuel company, and on the argument that some of these companies have known for years the consequences of their activities and instead of addressing it, they withheld evidence, spread misinformation, and kept increasing their production. One of the first lawsuits for damage occurred in 2015, with the State of New York accusing Exxon Mobil Corporation of deceiving investors about the company's management of risks posed by climate change regulation, alleging a fraudulent scheme against shareholders. Later in 2018, the State of New York filed another lawsuit against Exxon, accusing the company of having hidden for years internal research that demonstrated the direct causal link between fossil fuels and climate change. Since then, several cities and counties have filed civil lawsuits against dozens of oil companies around the United States. In 2023 the state of California sued the major fossil fuel companies, making it the largest jurisdiction taking legal action against them.

Climate litigation cases to compensate individuals also began around the same time. For instance, in 2018, associations representing a California crab fishermen filed suit against 30 fossil fuel companies seeking to make the companies pay for the harm global warming has caused to California's fisheries[3]. The suit demanded that petroleum firms compensate monetarily for the changes that will be needed to sustain the crab fishing industry in the future. In 2017 a Peruvian farmer sued the German energy giant RWE for contributing to climate change[4]. He claimed damages from RWE to protect his hometown of Huaraz from a swollen glacier lake at risk of overflowing from melting snow and ice, a legal battle he initiated with the NGO Germanwatch. At first instance the judges rejected the request of the South American farmer and mountain guide, but once appealed the regional High Court ruled the request for compensation was admissible. The ruling was historical, because it created legal precedent for the link between climate disasters and emissions of individual fossil fuel companies, making the principle of attribution science legally valid, even between distant jurisdictions.

Attribution Science

Using Attribution Science it is possible to calculate with a certain scientific accuracy the contributing share of each individual fossil fuel company for climate catastrophes. Attribution Science[5] was born in 2017, when the scientific journal "Climatic Change" published a study by the American climatologist Brenda Ekwurzel and some of her colleagues from the non-profit organization Union of Concerned Scientists. The study demonstrated the percentage in which the ninety main carbon dioxide producers in the world have contributed to the increase in the concentration of carbon dioxide (CO_2) in the atmosphere. Using this methodology, climate scientists are now able to attribute the percentage of specific extreme events to companies with sufficient certainty, like to what extent ExxonMobil or Shell, BP, or ENI need to compensate those that are affected by climate damage. For instance, it has been calculated that the company RWE has contributed to approximately 0.5% of emissions caused by human activity from the Industrial Revolution up until today. Consequently, a farmer in Peru can claim financial compensation for the CO2 emissions resulting from RWE's mining and burning of lignite and other types of coal for German electric power production.

In 2023 a new study was released indicating that the world's top fossil fuel companies owe at least $209bn a year in climate reparations to compensate communities suffering the most harm from climate change[6]. Specifically, the peer-reviewed paper proposed that the top 21 polluting companies pay $5.4 trillion over the next 25 years to compensate for climate damages[7].

References

Seminal climate lawsuits in the United States:
• State of California v. BP, ExxonMobil, Chevron, Shell and ConocoPhillips and their trade group, the American Petroleum Institute, 2023
• County of Multnomah v. Exxon Mobil Corp. 2023
• Municipalities of Puerto Rico v. Exxon Mobil Corp. 2022
• City of New York v. Exxon Mobil Corp., 2021
• City & County of Honolulu v. Sunoco LP, 2020
• Rhode Island v. Shell Oil Products Co., 2018
• City of New York v. BP p.l.c., 2018
• City of Oakland v. BP p.l.c., 2017
• County of San Mateo v. Chevron Corp, and at All, 2017
• County of Santa Cruz v. Chevron Corp. and at All, 2017
• People of the State of New York v. Exxon Mobil Corporation, 2015

Currently, there are more than twenty legal cases underway in the U.S. to make fossil fuel companies pay for climate disasters. Hundreds of international legal cases can be found in the Climate Change Litigation Databases by Columbia University in New York.

Notes

1. A Dutch environmental group, the Urgenda Foundation, alongside 900 Dutch citizens, sued the Dutch government to require it to do more to prevent global climate change. The court in the Hague ordered the Dutch state to limit GHG emissions to 25% below 1990 levels by 2020, finding the government's existing pledge to reduce emissions by 17% insufficient to meet the state's fair contribution toward the UN goal of keeping global temperature increases within two degrees Celsius of pre-industrial conditions.

2. "Court orders Royal Dutch Shell to cut carbon emissions by 45% by 2030. Oil giant told plans should be brought into line with Paris climate agreement". From the Guardian, May, 2021.

3. "Crab fishermen sue 30 oil firms over climate change". From the Guardian, November, 2018.

4. "Peruvian farmer sues German energy giant for contributing to climate change". From Agence France-Presse, November 14, 2017.

5. Historically the 2004 paper entitled "Human Contribution to the European Heat Wave of 2003" is generally considered to be the first attribution science study. However, the use of the term attribution science was only popularized with the release of the Carbon Majors database in 2017.

6. "Fossil Fuel Companies Should Pay Trillions in 'Climate Reparations,' New Study Argues". From Inside Climate News, May, 2023.

7. "Time to pay the piper: Fossil fuel companies' reparations for climate damages" by Marco Grasso and Richard Heede, from One Earth, N5, P459-463, May 19, 2023.

Carbon Majors

Carbon Majors are defined as the largest corporations or entities that contribute to global carbon dioxide (CO_2) emissions. The Climate Accountability Institute was founded in 2013, and in 2017 it published the Carbon Majors Database, which was the first historical data release indicating the estimated amount of greenhouse gasses emitted by each major fossil fuel company in the world since the beginning of the Industrial Revolution. It originally contained 90 companies producing coal, oil, gas, and cement dating back to 1854, and it showed that fossil fuel producers are responsible for nearly 1 trillion tons of greenhouse emissions. The estimates were possible through aggregating data from the International Energy Agency (IEA) and several other sources.

From the full Carbon Major Database, a specific dataset focuses on the emissions from 100 producers over the period 1988-2015. This is a symbolic timeframe because 1988 was the year of formation of the Intergovernmental Panel on Climate Change (IPCC) and when climate change was largely recognized by the political arena, the media, the general public, and the fossil fuel industry as well. This dataset deduced that the 100 major oil, gas, and coal producers have generated over 70% of greenhouse emissions.

Among the Carbon Majors, it is important to note that they can be totally or partially private international oil companies, commonly known as IOCs (International Oil Companies), or public national companies, defined as NOCs (National Oil Companies). Companies such as ExxonMobil, ENI, and Shell are included among the IOCs. However, state giants such as PetroChina, Gazprom, and Saudi Aramco are part of the NOCs. The difference between NOCs and IOCs also refers to the type of legal liability and jurisdictions that can hold them accountable, however, these companies are often transnational with subsidiaries and headquarters across most countries worldwide. It is important to note that these companies form partnerships, merge, or trade their assets. For example, the French company Total had contracts with the Russian company Novatek. It is also important to note that multiple companies often fall under the jurisdiction of the same regulatory framework. This is evident in the case of European firms and those in the United States, which, when totaled together, account for the majority of emissions produced worldwide.

Top 100 Carbon Majors
Percentage of CO2 emissions 1988-2015

1	China (Coal)	14.32%
2	Saudi Arabian Oil Company (Aramco)	4.50%
3	Gazprom OAO	3.91%
4	National Iranian Oil Co	2.28%
5	ExxonMobil Corp	1.98%
6	Coal India	1.87%
7	Petroleos Mexicanos (Pemex)	1.87%
8	Russia (Coal)	1.86%
9	Royal Dutch Shell PLC	1.67%
10	China National Petroleum Corp (CNPC)	1.56%
11	BP PLC	1.53%
12	Chevron Corp	1.31%
13	Petroleos de Venezuela SA (PDVSA)	1.23%
14	Abu Dhabi National Oil Co	1.20%
15	Poland Coal	1.16%
16	Peabody Energy Corp	1.15%
17	Sonatrach SPA	1.00%
18	Kuwait Petroleum Corp	1.00%
19	Total SA	0.95%
20	BHP Billiton Ltd	0.91%
21	ConocoPhillips	0.91%
22	Petroleo Brasileiro SA (Petrobras)	0.77%
23	Lukoil OAO	0.75%
24	Rio Tinto	0.75%
25	Nigerian National Petroleum Corp	0.72%
26	Petroliam Nasional Berhad (Petronas)	0.69%
27	Rosneft OAO	0.65%
28	Arch Coal Inc	0.63%
29	Iraq National Oil Co	0.60%
30	Eni SPA	0.59%
31	Anglo American	0.59%
32	Surgutneftegas OAO	0.57%
33	Alpha Natural Resources Inc	0.54%
34	Qatar Petroleum Corp	0.54%

35	PT Pertamina	0.54%
36	Kazakhstan Coal	0.53%
37	Statoil ASA	0.52%
38	National Oil Corporation of Libya	0.50%
39	Consol Energy Inc	0.50%
40	Ukraine Coal	0.49%
41	RWE AG	0.47%
42	Oil & Natural Gas Corp Ltd	0.40%
43	Glencore PLC	0.38%
44	TurkmenGaz	0.36%
45	Sasol Ltd	0.35%
46	Repsol SA	0.33%
47	Anadarko Petroleum Corp	0.33%
48	Egyptian General Petroleum Corp	0.31%
49	Petroleum Development Oman LLC	0.31%
50	Czech Republic Coal	0.30%
51	China Petrochemical Corp (Sinopec)	0.29%
52	China National Offshore Oil Corp Ltd (CNOOC)	0.28%
53	Ecopetrol SA	0.27%
54	Singareni Collieries Company	0.27%
55	Occidental Petroleum Corp	0.26%
56	Sonangol EP	0.26%
57	Tatneft OAO	0.23%
58	North Korea Coal	0.23%
59	Bumi Resources	0.23%
60	Suncor Energy Inc	0.22%
61	Petoro AS	0.21%
62	Devon Energy Corp	0.20%
63	Natural Resource Partners LP	0.19%
64	Marathon Oil Corp	0.19%
65	Vistra Energy	0.19%
66	Encana Corp	0.18%
67	Canadian Natural Resources Ltd	0.17%
68	Hess Corp	0.16%

69	Exxaro Resources Ltd	0.16%
70	YPF SA	0.15%
71	Apache Corp	0.15%
72	Murray Coal	0.15%
73	Alliance Resource Partners LP	0.15%
74	Syrian Petroleum Co	0.15%
75	Novatek OAO	0.14%
76	NACCO Industries Inc	0.13%
77	KazMunayGas	0.13%
78	Adaro Energy PT	0.13%
79	Petroleos del Ecuador	0.12%
80	Inpex Corp	0.12%
81	Kiewit Mining Group	0.12%
82	AP Moller (Maersk)	0.11%
83	Banpu Public Co Ltd	0.11%
84	EOG Resources Inc	0.11%
85	Husky Energy Inc	0.11%
86	Kideco Jaya Agung PT	0.10%
87	Bahrain Petroleum Co (BAPCO)	0.10%
88	Westmoreland Coal Co	0.10%
89	Cloud Peak Energy Inc	0.10%
90	Chesapeake Energy Corp	0.10%
91	Drummond Co	0.09%
92	Teck Resources Ltd	0.09%
93	Turkmennebit	0.07%
94	OMV AG	0.06%
95	Noble Energy Inc	0.06%
96	Murphy Oil Corp	0.06%
97	Berau Coal Energy Tbk PT	0.06%
98	Bukit Asam (Persero) Tbk PT	0.05%
99	Indika Energy Tbk PT	0.04%
100	Southwestern Energy Co	0.04%

CLIMATE CLASS ACTION

Climate Class Action

In the *Climate Class Action* project, major fossil fuel companies are accused of causing personal damages resulting from floods, droughts, wildfires, hurricanes, heatwaves, coastal erosion, and other consequences of climate breakdown.

Cirio created the website *ClimateClassAction.com* to advocate for class action suits against major fossil fuel firms. His platform empowers individuals to estimate financial compensation for personal climate damage, and strives to foster community among people affected by the climate crisis.

For this project, Cirio has compiled a comprehensive list of accusations, evidence, legal case studies, and news articles, all of which are shared on the website. The online campaign utilizes social media posts and videos to inform citizens about their right to seek compensation for climate disasters, generating dialogue within the realm of climate litigation and climate justice.

A class action is a legal lawsuit filed on behalf of a group of individuals who have suffered similar harm or injuries caused by the same entity or situation. Instead of each person individually pursuing legal action, they join together as a class, allowing for more efficient and cost-effective resolution of their claims.

The Accusations Against the Fossil Fuel Industry

Fossil fuel companies owe billions of dollars to citizens whose lives and belongings have been damaged or lost forever. *ClimateClassAction.com* wants to provide an unbiased and non-partisan service to citizens by allowing them to know their rights, to organize class action suits, and simulate claims for their personal damages. Despite the ongoing surge of climate-related lawsuits globally, there still hasn't been a class action dedicated to all citizens. People affected by climate disasters can now get together to sue the major fossil fuel companies in the United States and abroad.

For decades, fossil fuel companies have known about the consequences of their carbon emissions. However, they misinformed the public while making staggering profit, and destroying any opportunities for greener energy. These firms are directly responsible for climate disasters, and the damages they inflict on the personal life of citizens. Soaring greenhouse gas emissions have resulted in, and will continue to result in, a significant increase in the number and severity of extreme weather events, including floods and landslides, hurricanes and coastal erosion, heat waves and drought, wildfires and increased air pollution, and exacerbation of the spread of infectious diseases. These events also trigger economic inflation, hunger, mass migration, civil wars, and mass mortality.

Paolo Cirio compiled a list of accusations against fossil fuel firms by researching news articles, publications, documentaries, legal cases, and conversing with journalists, economists, and activists. These accusations are popularized through the *Climate Tribunal* series and are detailed in the following pages.

WHY FOSSIL FUEL COMPANIES ARE LEGALLY RESPONSIBLE

- *THEY LIED*

- *THEY KNEW*

- *THEY CAUSED DAMAGE*

- *THEY DIDN'T INNOVATE*

- *THEY MISLED THE PUBLIC*

- *THEY MISLED INVESTORS*

- *THEY DON'T PAY REPAIRS*

- *THEY CORRUPT POLITICS*

- *THEY POLLUTED THE MOST*

- *THEY MADE RECORD PROFIT*

• THEY LIED

The fossil fuel industry has perpetrated a multi-decade, multi-billion dollar disinformation, propaganda, and lobbying campaign to delay climate action by deceiving the public and policymakers about the climate crisis and its solutions. This has involved a remarkable number of advertisements in which fossil fuel firms have run climate denial messages on television, newspapers, and the Internet. After having denied the existence of climate change and their role in causing it, they kept spreading misleading advertising by promoting fossil fuels as integral to "climate solutions" without disclosing that fossil fuels are in fact the primary cause of climate change. In waging these deceptive advertising campaigns, fossil fuel firms are intentionally depriving consumers of information that is key to their purchase decisions.

• THEY KNEW

Major fossil fuel companies have been aware of the consequences of greenhouse emissions for more than half a century. Scientists have been warning governments about global warming due to the burning of fossil fuels and its consequences for society since the 1960s. Companies like Exxon and Shell internally commissioned studies in the early 1980s that assessed the effects of their greenhouse gas emissions. These studies already precisely established that the emissions from their products would generate a surge in global temperatures causing hurricanes, sea level rise, drought, floods, wildfires and many other climate calamities; they even predicted mass migrations and social unrest resulting from global warming. The documents of these scientific studies commissioned by the fossil fuel firms remained secret for decades, as they failed to disclose material facts intentionally, knowingly, and recklessly.

• THEY CAUSED DAMAGE

The economic damage of the climate crisis is skyrocketing. In 2022 alone, extreme weather caused 18 disasters costing the U.S. $165 billion. However these figures don't consider real estate losses, the disruption of supply chains, and increased scarcity of resources, including water. Besides personal harm, there are business damages that affect a variety of industries and related services, resulting in rising inflation, while huge losses are generated by ruining real estate, properties, infrastructures, and equipment. The whole world economy is at risk, while the fossil fuel firms make staggering profits, sheltering them in tax havens and in countries less affected by climate change. The economic damage caused by fossil fuel firms will impact everyone – while the governments and citizens pay losses, the gains are not taxed and reinvested in mitigation and adaptation.

• THEY DIDN'T INNOVATE

For decades the fossil fuel firms haven't innovated their technology to emit less greenhouse emissions, even though they were well aware of their consequences, nor have they developed new renewable energy production. Instead they have engaged in price fixing to speculate on fossil fuel supply by forming cartels and controlling business and trade organizations like OPEC. They have marketed themselves as clean innovative companies with the goal of attracting new consumers to their fossil fuel products, while blocking cleaner alternatives that contribute substantially less to climate change. The majority of their investments is in extracting and producing fossil fuels, as they monopolize the energy industry by acquiring patents, technologies, and projects for renewable energy alternatives just to keep them out of the market and not developing them, as it would be less profitable.

• THEY MISLED THE PUBLIC

The largest oil and gas companies and their top industry trade associations have systematically and intentionally misled consumers about the central role their products play in the climate crisis. Moreover, they mislead consumers with green-washing advertisements designed to represent their companies as environmentally responsible, focused on developing green technology and products, while in reality their investment in clean energy sources is minuscule, and their business models continue to center on the fossil fuel products driving climate change. They have nevertheless engaged in a coordinated, multi-front effort to conceal and deny their own knowledge of the damage they cause, discredit the growing body of publicly available scientific evidence, and persistently create doubt in the minds of customers, consumers, regulators, the media, journalists, teachers, and the public about the reality and consequences of the impact of their fossil fuel pollution. Their deception is effective, as fossil fuel companies are making massive profits, which in turn has enabled the unabated and expanded extraction, production, marketing, and sale of fossil fuels.

• THEY MISLED INVESTORS

The fossil fuel industry has misled investors by presenting false and misleading assurances that it effectively manages economic risks posed to its business by climate change regulations, lawsuits, and consequent fines and legal costs. Moreover, they misled investors about the risk of 'stranded assets' of fossil fuels reserves, and how the whole fossil fuel industry might collapse in favor of demand for more renewable energy. These potential massive losses in revenues and share value can affect investors. Shareholders include pension funds, municipalities, states, and other public stakeholders, which might be affected by mass losses because of the misleading financial projections by the fossil fuel industry. Misrepresentations and omissions of real, tangible facts as described here constitute actual fraud. Investors might suffer damages in connection with purchasing and retaining financial derivatives that were the direct and proximate result of fossil fuel firms' fraud.

• THEY DON'T PAY TO REPAIR

Instead of helping to clean up and compensate those affected by their products, the fossil fuel firms deny their accountability, aggressively avoiding their responsibility in fixing and paying for the damages caused by their products. They fight legal litigations that would make them pay and don't have insurance that would cover the damages caused. They fight carbon taxes that create revenues to repair, help, and compensate for the losses and damage they cause. Lately fossil fuel firms are initiating projects for decarbonization and carbon capture of their products by asking for public investment from governments at taxpayers' expense. Yet, these technologies for decarbonization and greenhouse gas capture are not efficient, and they shouldn't be economically exploited by the same companies that have interest in lowering the cost of production of the same emissions they generate.

• THEY CORRUPT POLITICS

Fossil fuel companies have lobbied to avoid regulation of their emissions and industries. During political elections, they fund parties and politicians who are against regulating or taxing greenhouse emissions, while corrupting politicians around the world to get permits and licenses to find and extract fossil fuels. They lobby even inside the same institutions dedicated to tackling climate change; in fact the fossil fuel firms were not questioned or even mentioned by the World Bank nor the IMF, international climate agreements, nor by anyone over the course of decades of negotiations and policymaking during UN and COP conferences. This corruption reached its disgraceful apex in 2023, with the presidency of COP being held by an oil company executive.

• THEY POLLUTED THE MOST

The 100 major oil, gas, and coal producers have generated over 70% of greenhouse gas emissions, making them the greatest threat to citizens and society as whole. The historical study Carbon Major Database by the Climate Accountability Institute determined precise responsibilities each international fossil fuel firm has. The cumulative greenhouse emissions by the major fossil fuel firms in the United States, Europe, and United Kingdom are approximately 20% of the total emitted worldwide. China accounts for 17%, Russia 9%, and the Middle East 14%. These statistics prove that companies from the U.S., U.K., and E.U. maintain a great amount of responsibility for having triggered the climate crisis. Furthermore, the trade of fossil fuel has been driven by western countries, which acquired licenses to extract fossil fuel or buy it from foreign countries. Therefore, despite the origin of extraction, the greater amount of emissions comes from the production and consumption of fossil fuels by western countries. For instance, the United States has emitted a quarter of the total world greenhouse gasses, more than any other country.

• THEY MADE RECORD PROFIT

The oil sector alone made astounding profits at the dizzying rate of $3 Billion-a-Day for many decades. Meanwhile, the fossil fuel industry receives public subsidies of $11 Million-a-Minute and often billions in tax breaks or isn't taxed at all. In addition, the biggest banks in the world have provided billions to the oil, gas, and coal firms as investment in new extraction of fossil fuel. Recently, in 2022, fossil fuel firms made record profits. ExxonMobil reported record $20 billion quarterly profit, and Shell posted almost $10 billion, and yet they are still investing more money in new fossil fuel extraction, despite net zero pledges.

HISTORY OF THE POLITICAL ECONOMY OF CLIMATE CHANGE

History of the Political Economy of Climate Change

The political economic history of climate change traces the role of the fossil fuels industry's economic and political influence that contributed to global warming. Throughout the 20th century, the fossil fuel industry, the White House, and the media each played roles in acknowledging climate change and influencing policy-making, by both responding to concerns and engaging in denial regarding global warming. In addition to the rise in temperature and quantity of greenhouse emissions, political and economic interests have played a significant role in the history of climate change.

Some key political actors in this timeline include the White House as the most influential institution in addressing concerns for global warming, while United Nations' organizations were dedicated to scientific monitoring and participating in international negotiations. In terms of economic history, the main actor was the petroleum industry's major trade association, the American Petroleum Institute (API), in collaboration with individual companies such as Exxon, Chevron, BP, Shell, and Koch. As a further historical actor, the media, such as the New York Times, influenced public opinion and the political debate surrounding climate change.

Some of the key years included 1954, which saw a turning point when the American Petroleum Institute (API) acknowledged that burning fossil fuels caused global warming. Another significant year was 1965, when the U.S. President Lyndon Johnson warned of global warming in Congress. During the 1970s, several major fossil fuel firms commissioned research without denying their findings. It was 1988 when the fossil fuel industry began adopting an aggressive denial approach, just after the first policies to limit CO_2 emissions by the White House were implemented, and the United Nations established the IPCC. In 1989, fifty fossil fuel companies began to conspire together to derail regulations and scientific studies by forming the Global Climate Coalition (GCC). In 1995 the GCC made a plan to distort the political debate around the Kyoto Protocol, the first major international effort to slow global climate change, a plan that eventually succeeded. It's important to note that more than 50% of greenhouse gasses were emitted after the 1990, with the acceleration of the U.S. economic model, after the dissolution of the Soviet Union and Chinese economic reform.

The fossil fuel industry remains the main historical actor shaping politics, regulations, and education on the dangers of their activity, with the goal of expanding fossil fuel production and consumption. This history is mostly unknown and not taught in schools, featured in cultural works, or reported in the mainstream media due to decades-long communication strategies and influential soft power exerted by the fossil fuel industry. Nonetheless, some of this historical evidence is being utilized in climate litigation against fossil fuel firms and governments.

Paolo Cirio compiled this timeline by comparing various articles and publications. Revelations about the early knowledge of climate change by the fossil fuels industry began emerging only in 2015. To keep this history updated, Cirio shared the timeline as an open database, allowing researchers, historians, activists, lawyers, and journalists to use and contribute to it.

100 YEARS OF POLITICAL ECONOMIC HISTORY OF CLIMATE CHANGE, 1912 - 2012

1912
June 14
COURIER NEWS

The newspaper Plainfield Courier-News in New Jersey published the headline "Coal Consumption Affecting Climate" and mentioned in the article that the coal burned in furnaces around the world was causing an effect that "may be considerable in a few centuries". The same news was also found in newspapers in Australia and New Zealand. The source of the news was an article in the magazine Popular Mechanics published in March, 1912, which captured the basics of carbon dioxide (CO_2) impact on climate.

The news article indicated that "The furnaces of the world are now burning about 2,000,000,000 tons of coal a year" and that "when this is burned, uniting with oxygen, it adds about 7,000,000,000 tons of carbon dioxide to the atmosphere yearly. This tends to make the air a more effective blanket for the earth and to raise its temperature. The effect may be considerable in a few centuries." This article was titled "Remarkable Weather of 1911: The Effect of the Combustion of Coal on the Climate – What Scientists Predict for the Future" published on August 14, 1912, in a New Zealand newspaper.

Reference document:
"Coal Consumption Affecting Climate" newspaper Plainfield Courier-News, New Jersey, Friday, June 14, 1912.

Reference quote:
archive.nytimes.com/dotearth.blogs.nytimes.com/2016/10/21/coals-link-to-global-warming-explained-in-1912/

1919
March 20
API

The American Petroleum Institute (API) was established on March 20, 1919, in New York City and moved to Washington DC in late 1969. The API is the largest trade association for the oil and gas industry, representing over 600 corporate members, "from the largest major oil company to the smallest of independents, coming from all segments of the industry." The API was created following the antitrust lawsuits against John D. Rockefeller's Standard Oil in 1911, which resulted in its division into 34 separate companies. Many of these companies have since split, folded, or merged; today, the primary descendants of Standard Oil include ExxonMobil, Chevron, and ConocoPhillips.

API's mission has been to "influence public policy in support of a strong, viable U.S. oil and natural gas industry." According to API's website, it "speaks for the oil and natural gas industry to the public, Congress, the Executive Branch, state governments, and the media. We negotiate with regulatory agencies, represent the industry in legal proceedings, participate in coalitions, and work in partnership with other associations to achieve our members' public policy goals."

Reference document:
"Climate Disinformation Database, American Petroleum Institute", DeSmog.

Reference quote:
api.org/about

1931

EDISON

Thomas Edison envisioned using and storing what is now called renewable energy. Edison also suggested investing in solar energy generated with solar panels as he was skeptical of energy from burning fossil fuels. In 1931, not long before he died, the inventor told his friends Henry Ford and Harvey Firestone: "I'd put my money on the sun and solar energy. What a source of power! I hope we don't have to wait until oil and coal run out before we tackle that."

Already in an interview in 1910, Thomas Edison stated: "We should utilize natural forces and thus get all of our power. Sunshine is a form of energy, and the winds and the tides are manifestations of energy", adding "some day some fellow will invent a way of concentrating and storing up sunshine to use instead of this old, absurd Prometheus scheme of fire."

Reference document:
"Uncommon Friends: Life with Thomas Edison, Henry Ford, Harvey Firestone" book by James Newton. 1989.

Reference quote:
w with Thomas Edison in the magazine "The Fra" by the publisher Elbert Hubbard. Philistines and Roycrofters c.1 v.5, 1910.

1953
May 24
NEW YORK TIMES

The Canadian physicist Gilbert Plass talked at a scientific meeting about the dangers of carbon dioxide pollution. He made a sensational statement that became headline news around the world, including the New York Times. Plass stated: "The large increase in industrial activity during the present century is discharging so much carbon dioxide into the atmosphere that the average temperature is rising at the rate of 1.5 degrees per century." In 1961, he went further and blamed fossil fuels for most of the global warming.

The New York Times article wrote: "The amount of carbon dioxide in the air will double by the year 2080 and raise the temperature an average of at least 4 per cent. The burning of about two billion tons of coal and oil a year keeps the average ground temperature somewhat higher than it would otherwise be."

Reference document:
"On the Influence of Carbonic Acid in the Air upon the Temperature of the Ground",
Philosophical Magazine and Journal of Science Series 5, Vol 41. April 1896.

Reference quote:
nytimes.com/1953/05/24/archives/how-industry-may-change-climate.html

1954

API

The American Petroleum Institute (API) approved a research proposal by geochemist Harrison Brown and his colleagues at the California Institute of Technology (Caltech). The results indicated that fossil fuels had caused atmospheric CO_2 concentrations to rise by about 5% over the past century. In 1955, the API began funding the proposed research at Caltech under the name Project 53. Also in 1954, the Air Pollution Foundation, with links to API and several other major energy and automobile companies, funded in the Caltech's lab the research of Charles David Keeling to gather carbon dioxide samples, resulting in the famous Keeling's curve.

An excerpt from the research proposal to the API from Harrison Brown and colleagues in 1954: "Perhaps the most interesting effect concerning carbon in trees which we have thus far observed is a marked and fairly steady increase in the C_{12}/C_{13} ratio with time. Since 1840 the ratio has clearly increased markedly. This effect can be explained on the basis of a changing carbon dioxide concentration in the atmosphere resulting from industrialization and the consequent burning of large quantities of coal and petroleum. If this explanation were correct, the carbon dioxide content of the atmosphere today would be about 5% greater than it was a century ago." In November 1954, another Caltech research project at Brown's lab, funded by the Air Pollution Foundation and proposed by Keeling's director, Samuel Epstein, emphasized the potential impact on earth's climate of burning "coal and petroleum."

Reference document:
"The determination of the variations and causes of variations of the isotopic composition of carbon in nature" by Harrison Brown, California Institute of Technology, 1954.

Reference quote:
desmog.com/2024/01/30/fossil-fuel-industry-sponsored-climate-science-1954-keeling-api-wspa/

1955

FORD

The physicist Gilbert Plass joined the advanced research staff at the Aeronutronic division of the Ford Motor Company. In 1960, he became manager of the research lab at Ford's theoretical physics department. Gilbert Plass published a series of eye-grabbing pieces on climate, including a 1956 article published in the magazine American Scientist titled "Carbon Dioxide and the Climate" and in a paper in the journal Tellus titled "The Carbon Dioxide Theory of Climatic Change."

Reference document:
"Carbon Dioxide and the Climate" by Gilbert Plass, American Scientist, 1956.

1957

EXXON

Humble Oil (now Exxon) scientists, led by H.R. Brannon, published a report that not only acknowledged the increasing levels of atmospheric CO_2 but also recognized the clear contribution of fossil fuels to this rise. Humble's researchers studied the fingerprints of fossil fuel emissions in the wood of growing trees. Humble Oil and Refining Co. was an American oil company founded in 1911 in Humble, Texas. In 1919, a 50% share in Humble was acquired by Standard Oil of New Jersey (Exxon), after the fall of John D. Rockefeller's empire.

The New York Times quoted Center for International Environmental Law (CIEL) director Carroll Muffett on the stunning implications of these documents: "From 1957 onward, there is no doubt that Humble Oil, which is now Exxon, was clearly on notice" about rising CO_2 in the atmosphere and the prospect that it was likely to cause global warming.

Reference document:
"Humble Oil Company Radiocarbon Dates II" by H. R. Brannon, Jr., L. H. Simons, D. Perry, A. C. Daughtry, and E. McFarlan, Vol 125, Issue 3254. May 10, 1957.

Reference quote:
nytimes.com/2016/04/14/science/pressure-on-exxon-over-climate-change-intensifies-with-new-documents.html

1958

SHELL

Charles Jones identified himself as both the executive secretary of the Smoke and Fumes Committee as well as an executive with Shell. In a document, Jones reported that the Committee was funding a study at Truesdail Laboratories to "determine the amount of carbon of fossil origin" in the atmosphere.

In a presentation on behalf of the Smoke and Fumes Committee to the government-convened National Conference on Air Pollution later that same year, Jones stated: "The petroleum industry supplies the fuel used by the automobile, and thus has a sincere interest in the solution to the problem of pollution from automobile exhaust. The stated objective of the Smoke and Fumes Committee of the American Petroleum Institute is to determine the causes and methods of control of objectionable atmospheric pollution resulting from the production, manufacture, transportation, sale, and use of petroleum and its products."

Reference document:
"Sources of Air Pollution: Transportation (Petroleum)". Presentation at the National Conference on Air Pollution by Charles A. Jones. November 19, 1958.

1959
November 4
API

Physicist Edward Teller spoke about global warming that could melt the ice caps and submerge coastal cities at an oil industry symposium organized by the American Petroleum Institute (API) in the symposium called "Energy and Man" at the Columbia Graduate School of Business to commemorate the centennial of the oil industry in the United States. Over 300 government officials, economists, historians, scientists, and industry executives were present for Dr. Teller's talk. He was a guest of honor for a grand occasion: the centennial of the American oil industry.

Edward Teller, on November 4, 1959, addressed the crowd in his presentation "Energy Patterns of the Future" and his words carried a warning: "Whenever you burn conventional fuel, you create carbon dioxide. [...] Carbon dioxide has a strange property. It transmits visible light but it absorbs the infrared radiation which is emitted from the earth. Its presence in the atmosphere causes a greenhouse effect [...] It has been calculated that a temperature rise corresponding to a 10 percent increase in carbon dioxide will be sufficient to melt the ice caps and submerge New York. All the coastal cities would be covered, and since a considerable percentage of the human race lives in coastal regions, I think that this chemical contamination is more serious than most people tend to believe."

Reference document:
"Energy Patterns of The Future" by Edward Teller.

Reference quote:
greenoptimistic.com/edward-teller-global-warming-20180109/

1961

OPEC

Because of the Anglo-American dominance in the oil economy, in 1961, The Organization of Petroleum Exporting Countries (OPEC) was formed, initially by Saudi Arabia, Iraq, Kuwait, Iran, and Venezuela to protect the sovereignty of each country's natural resources. It has since included Algeria, Angola, the Republic of the Congo, Equatorial Guinea, Gabon, Libya, Nigeria, and the United Arab Emirates.

Reference document:
"Organization of the Petroleum Exporting Countries (OPEC)", Wikipedia entry.

1962

SHELL

Shell's chief geologist, Houston-based Marion King Hubbert, produced a book-length report on energy for the U.S. National Academy of Sciences that explicitly warned of the risks human-induced global warming could pose to earth's weather and "ecological balances."

Shell geologist Marion King Hubbert explicitly warned about the risks of man-made climate change, writing: "There is evidence that the increasing use of the fossil fuels [...] is contaminating the earth's atmosphere with CO_2. [...] It is possible that this is already producing a secular climatic change in the direction of higher average temperatures."

Reference document:
"A Crack in the Shell: New Documents Expose a Hidden Climate History" by The Center for International Environmental Law, April, 2018.

1963

WHITE HOUSE

The Clean Air Act (CAA) is the United States' primary federal air quality law, intended to reduce and control air pollution nationwide. Initially enacted in 1963 and amended many times since, it is one of the United States' first and most influential modern environmental laws.

The Clean Air Act of 1963 was the first federal legislation to permit the U.S. federal government to take direct action to control air pollution. It extended the 1955 research program, encouraging cooperative state, local, and federal action to reduce air pollution.

Reference document:
Clean Air Act, Pub. L. Tooltip Public Law, United States, 88–206. 1963.

1965
November 5
WHITE HOUSE

United States' President Lyndon Johnson told Congress: "This generation has altered the composition of the atmosphere on a global scale through a steady increase in carbon dioxide from the burning of fossil fuels." In 1965 scientific advisors warned Johnson about climate change with a report by the Science Advisory Committee. The report contained an entire section discussing carbon dioxide from fossil fuels, which is described as "the invisible pollutant."

President Lyndon Johnson's Science Advisory Committee found that "pollutants have altered on a global scale the carbon dioxide content of the air" and "man is unwittingly conducting a vast geophysical experiment" by burning fossil fuels that are injecting CO_2 into the atmosphere. The committee concludes that by the year 2000, we could see "measurable and perhaps marked changes in climate, and will almost certainly cause significant changes in the temperature and other properties of the stratosphere."

Reference document:
"Restoring the Quality of our Environment". Report of the Environmental Pollution Panel, President's Science Advisory Committee (PSAC).

Reference quote:
climatefiles.com/climate-change-evidence/presidents-report-atmospher-carbon-dioxide/

1965

API

In a speech by the President of American Petroleum Institute (API), Frank Ikard, at a major oil industry conference, he described federal research into climate change spurred by fossil fuels, saying: "The substance of the report is that there is still time to save the world's people from the catastrophic consequence of pollution, but time is running out." He outlined the findings of a report by then-president Lyndon Johnson's Science Advisory Committee, based in part on research the institute conducted in the 1950s.

In a 1965 speech to members, American Petroleum Institute (API)'s President Frank Ikard stated that "one of the most important predictions of the report is that carbon dioxide is being added to the earth's atmosphere by the burning of coal, oil, and natural gas at such a rate that by the year 2000 the heat balance will be so modified as possibly to cause marked changes in climate beyond local or even national efforts."

Reference document:
"Meeting the Challenges of 1966" by the American Petroleum Institute. 1965.

Reference quote:
davidsuzuki.org/story/decades-of-denial-and-stalling-have-created-a-climate-crunch/

1966
August
COAL INDUSTRY

In the industry publication Mining Congress Journal, James R. Garvey, who was the President of Bituminous Coal Research Inc. stated "changes in temperature will cause melting of the polar ice caps, which, in turn, would result in the inundation of many coastal cities, including New York and London" as a result of the combustion of fossil fuels, and particularly the use of coal.

James R. Garvey, who was the President of Bituminous Coal Research Inc., a now-defunct coal mining and processing research organization wrote: "There is evidence that the amount of carbon dioxide in the earth's atmosphere is increasing rapidly as a result of the combustion of fossil fuels" and "If the future rate of increase continues as it is at the present, it has been predicted that, because the CO_2 envelope reduces radiation, the temperature of the earth's atmosphere will increase and that vast changes in the climates of the earth will result", and in particular Garvey wrote "such changes in temperature will cause melting of the polar ice caps, which, in turn, would result in the inundation of many coastal cities, including New York and London."

Reference document:
"Air Pollution and the Coal Industry" by James Garvey, article in the Mining Congress Journal. August 1966.

1966

SHELL

On behalf of Shell, the British scientist and chemist James Lovelock conducted climate research during this period into the potential global consequences of air pollution caused by fossil fuels. The title of his report was "Combustion of Fossil Fuels: Large Scale Atmospheric Effects." In an unpublished essay written in 1966, Lovelock predicted that in the most likely scenario would see the world struck by an ecological disaster in the year 2000. Shell kept the results secret, asking Lovelock not to discuss them with "non-Shell people."

Chemist James Lovelock wrote in his essay "Some thoughts on the year 2000" commissioned by Shell: "The most probable of all curbs is the threat of an ecological disaster. That could most probably arise through the accumulation of harmful waste products." His conclusion: "What seems to be important is [...] the almost certain fact that the climate is worsening and the probability that the combustion of fuel is responsible."

Reference document:
"Some thoughts on the year 2000" by James Lovelock and "Combustion of Fossil Fuels: Large Scale Atmospheric Effects". National Science. Collection JEL. Novembre 11, 1966.

1967

UN

The International Council for Science (ICSU) and the World Meteorological Organization (WMO) launched the Global Atmospheric Research Programme (GARP) to better understand the behavior of the atmosphere and the physical basis of climate. The World Meteorological Organization is a specialized agency of the United Nations responsible for promoting international cooperation on atmospheric science, climatology, hydrology, and geophysics.

The aim of the Global Atmospheric Research Programme (GARP) was to improve the models used for weather forecasting, but eventually it would be drawn into the climate issue. In 1967, a study by S. Manabe and R.T. Wetherald of the Geophysical Fluid Dynamics Laboratory at Princeton, had noted that a doubling of the CO_2 content of the atmosphere would lead to an increase in global mean temperature of 2°C.

Reference document:
"Global Atmospheric Research Programme (GARP)", Wikipedia entry.

1967

API

The American Petroleum Institute (API) protested against a bill to promote the development of electric cars with the argument that governments should "stimulate all efforts by industry to eliminate automotive pollution, rather than dedicate federal funds to the promotion of any single possible solution."

Reference document:
"Oil industry has sought to block state backing for green tech since 1960s" article by Ajit Niranjan, The Guardian, 2024.

1968
February 1
API

The American Petroleum Institute (API) commissioned a report finding that: "Significant temperature changes are almost certain to occur by the year 2000, and these could bring about climatic changes." The research was written by Elmer Robinson and Bob Robbins, well known scientists at the Stanford Research Institute, known as SRI.

The paper commissioned by the American Petroleum Institute (API) and written by Elmer Robinson and Bob Robbins found that: "Although there are other possible sources for the additional CO_2 now being observed in the atmosphere, none seems to fit the presently observed situation as well as the fossil fuel emanation theory" and "significant temperature changes are almost certain to occur by the year 2000, and these could bring about climatic changes" concluding that "there seems to be no doubt that the potential damage to our environment could be severe." This paper – along with a follow-up that Robinson and Robbins produced in 1969 – play a key role in lawsuits seeking to hold oil companies accountable for climate change. The 1969 paper cited models predicting atmospheric CO_2 would reach 370 parts per million by 2000 – astonishingly close to the actual reading.

Reference document:
"Sources, Abundance, and Fate of Gaseous Atmospheric Pollutants" by Elmer Robinson and Bob Robbins, Stanford Research Institute.

Reference quote:
e360.yale.edu/features/climate-lawsuits-oil-industry-research

1970
January 1
WHITE HOUSE

The National Environmental Policy Act (NEPA) was signed into law on January 1, 1970. NEPA required federal agencies to assess the environmental effects of their proposed actions prior to making decisions. It promoted the enhancement of the environment and established the President's Council on Environmental Quality.

Reference document:
National Environmental Policy Act of 1969. Enacted by the 91st United States Congress.
Effective January 1, 1970.

1970
SHELL

Shell appeared to accept responsibility for harms caused by its products in an industry journal article. The Dutch trade publication Chemisch Weekblad (Chemical Weekly) published research into "chemistry and ethics" which included the results of interviews with executives of Shell who admitted responsibility for "annoying consequences" from global warming.

Representatives from Shell appeared to acknowledge that the company bore some responsibility for the problems that its products would cause, stating that: "If a product is used, as indicated by Shell, and annoying consequences nevertheless arise, Shell feels partly responsible."

Reference document:
Chemisch Weekblad. Verantwoordelijkheid in een chemisch bedrijf CW. October 23, 1970.

Reference quote:
ftm.eu/articles/new-shell-documents-could-aid-climate-cases-attorneys-say

1970

ENI

A report by the Italian oil company ENI's Isvet research center warned of the "catastrophic" risks from the build-up of carbon dioxide, CO2. The report made clear that left unchecked, rising fossil fuel use could lead to a climate crisis within just a few decades.

The study commissioned by ENI between 1969 and 1970 made clear that left unchecked, rising fossil fuel use would lead to a climate crisis within just a few decades with "catastrophic" risks. Despite knowing about the risks of its products since 1970, ENI, Italy's largest multinational company and one of seven "supermajor" oil firms in the world, used "lobbying and greenwashing" to push for more fossil fuels.

Reference document:
"L'intervento Pubblico Contro l'Inquinamento" by Gianni Scaiola.

Reference quote:
downtoearth.org.in/news/energy/italian-oil-major-eni-lobbied-for-more-fossil-fuels-despite-1970-internal-report-warning-of-dangers-faces-lawsuit-89428

1971
TOTAL

An internal magazine by the major French oil company Total explained that burning fossil fuels caused the release of "enormous amounts of carbon dioxide" in the atmosphere, the consequences of which were potentially "catastrophic". However the company, now rebranded as TotalEnergies, promoted doubt regarding the scientific basis for global warming by the late 1980s.

The article in the magazine Total Information mentioned that "since the 19th century, humans have been burning increasing amounts of fossil fuels. This results in the release of enormous quantities of carbon dioxide. [...] The overall amount of carbon dioxide present in the atmosphere, therefore, has increased significantly. [...] The increase has been around 15% over the last 150 years, which is not negligible. [...] If the consumption of coal and oil keeps the same rhythm in the years to come, the concentration of carbon dioxide will reach 400 parts per million around 2010."

Reference document:
"Atmospheric Pollution and Climate" by F. Durand-Dastès in Total Information N47, 1971.

Reference quote:
sciencedirect.com/science/article/pii/S0959378021001655

1971
WHITE HOUSE

Richard Nixon, President of the United States, imposed a price ceiling on oil in 1971 as demand increased and production declined. This led to greater dependence on foreign oil imports, as low prices boosted consumption. In 1973, Nixon announced the end of this quota system.

Reference document:
"The 1973 Oil Crisis", Wikipedia entry.

1973

ENI

The Italian oil company ENI studied pollution problems with its company Tecneco, formed in Rome in 1971. A report by Tecneco from 1973 predicted that human activities could "gradually cause the disappearance of all life on earth." Another section of the report stated that the "increase of carbon dioxide in the atmosphere is considered a potential cause of climate change."

The report on the company Tecneco by ENI mentioned that "this increase in concentration is quite worrying [...] carbon dioxide plays a large role in the thermal balance of the atmosphere [...] air richer in carbon dioxide absorbs more radiation and heats up. It is possible, therefore, that an increase in the average temperature of the atmosphere is to be feared. The calculated orders of magnitude are obviously small (from 1-1.5 °C) but could have important impacts. Atmospheric circulation could be modified, and it is not impossible, according to some, to foresee at least a partial melting of the polar ice caps, which would certainly result in significant sea level rise. The catastrophic consequences are easy to imagine."

Reference document:
"Prima relazione sulla situazione ambientale del Paese", TECNECO, Volume 1.

Reference quote:
desmog.com/2023/09/24/italian-oil-giant-eni-knew-about-climate-change-more-than-50-years-ago-report-reveals/

1973

WHITE HOUSE

After the international 1973 Oil Crisis, the petrodollar system was created through a deal between the U.S. and Saudi Arabia. As a result, other countries in the Middle East agreed to price and trade oil in U.S. dollars, so any country that purchased oil from Saudi Arabia would have to use U.S. dollars. The 1973 agreement was initiated by Richard Nixon, President of the United States, and the petrodollar is still in place today, making the U.S. dominant in global oil trade.

During the 1973 Arab-Israeli War, Arab members of the Organization of Petroleum Exporting Countries (OPEC) imposed an embargo against the United States in retaliation for the U.S. decision to resupply the Israeli military and gain leverage in the post-war peace negotiations. The spark of the embargo was the Yom Kippur War in October 1973, when a coalition of Arab states led by Egypt and Syria launched a surprise attack on Israel on the holiest day of the Jewish calendar.

Reference document:
"The 1973 Oil Crisis", Wikipedia entry.

1974

CHEVRON

Chevron obtained a patent for a method and apparatus for reducing ice forces on a marine structure prone to being frozen in ice through natural weather conditions, allowing for drilling in previously unreachable Arctic areas that would become seasonally accessible. In 1973 Exxon obtained a patent for a cargo ship capable of breaking through sea ice thanks to warmer temperatures. Shell obtained a patent similar to Exxon's in 1984.

Reference document:
"Chevron Research & Technology Co., Patent US3831385A: Arctic offshore platform"
granted on August 27, 1974. "Texaco Inc., Patent US3793840A: Mobile, arctic drilling
and production platform" granted on February 26, 1974.

1974
FORD

A Ford Foundation study drew the clear conclusion that global warming would become a major problem. In said scenario, the authors warned about the "complete melting of Arctic sea ice" and "widespread disruption of agriculture" as well as a rise in sea levels of "more than twenty feet (6m)". According to the authors, a possible solution would be a "zero energy growth" policy, which would make moving away from fossil fuels inevitable.

An investigation by E&E News revealed that scientists working at two of the largest American automakers had knowledge as far back as the 1960s that car emissions contributed to climate change. However the political lobbying by the two car giants Ford and General Motors undermined global attempts to reduce emissions while stalling U.S. efforts to make vehicles cleaner.

Reference document:
"A Time To Choose: America's Energy Future" by America's Ford Foundation. 1974.

Reference quote:
eenews.net/articles/exclusive-gm-ford-knew-about-climate-change-50-years-ago/

1975

GM

Ruth Annette Gabriel Reck, a researcher at the General Motors Research Laboratories was allowed by the GM's executives to publish her findings on climate change, including a paper in Science, where she asserted that aerosols caused "heating of the atmosphere near the poles." Reck left the automaker in 1992 after she was allegedly told to stop researching environmental issues.

Reference document:
"Aerosols and Polar Temperature Changes" by Ruth A. Reck. Science, New Series, Vol. 188, No. 4189, May 16, 1975.

1975

API

The American Petroleum Institute (API) opposed an energy saving bill that included refundable income tax credits for heat pumps in homes. "The United States has a large resource base of conventional energy such as oil, gas, and coal" it said, and that "expeditious development of these supplies can make a significant contribution not only to improving U.S. energy independence, but to create a healthy economy."

Reference document:
"Oil industry has sought to block state backing for green tech since 1960s" article by Ajit Niranjan, The Guardian, 2024.

1975
SHELL

A study partially funded and commissioned by Shell, stated that "increases in the CO_2 content of the atmosphere could lead to the so-called greenhouse effect [...] due to fossil fuel waste disposal [...] which would be enough to induce major climatic changes." Three years later, another report warned that "the continued burning of fossil fuels will lead to a manifold increase in the atmospheric CO_2 concentration."

Reference document:
"Dirty Pearls: Exposing Shell's hidden legacy of climate change accountability, 1970-1990" by Vatan Hüzeir. 2023.

1977
July
EXXON

Senior scientist James Black, top technical expert in Exxon's Research & Engineering division, delivered a sobering message to Exxon's Management Committee. He stated: "In the first place, there is general scientific agreement that the most likely manner in which mankind is influencing the global climate is through carbon dioxide release from the burning of fossil fuels." At the meeting at Exxon Corporation's headquarters, Exxon's leaders received this blunt assessment well before the climate crisis had become widely recognized.

Reference document:
Presentation shared with Exxon Management Committee from Exxon Research and Engineering Science Advisor, James Black.

1978

June 6

EXXON

A year after Exxon's Science Advisor, James Black, had warned the company's Management Committee about the dangers of climatic changes, he released an updated version of his presentation to a broader audience. He warned that a doubling of carbon dioxide (CO_2) concentration in the atmosphere could increase average global temperatures by 2 to 3 degrees Celsius, and by as much as 10 degrees Celsius at the poles. Rainfall might become heavier in some regions, while other places could turn into deserts.

James Black said, in the written summary of his talk, "some countries would benefit but others would have their agricultural output reduced or destroyed." Black estimated that quick action was needed. "Present thinking" he wrote in the summary, "holds that man has a time window of five to ten years before the need for hard decisions regarding changes in energy strategies might become critical."

Reference document:
"Exxon: The Road Not Taken" by John H. Cushman (Jr.), Neela Banerjee, David Hasemyer, Lisa Song. 2015.

Reference quote:
insideclimatenews.org/news/16092015/exxons-own-research-confirmed-fossil-fuels-role-in-global-warming/

1978
September 17
WHITE HOUSE

Congress passes the National Climate Policy Act to help "the Nation and the world to understand and respond to natural and man-induced climate processes and their implications."

Introduced in the U.S. Congress's House in 1976, the National Climate Program Act "directs the Secretary of Commerce to coordinate the establishment and operation of a Federal climate program for the collection, analysis, and dissemination of data concerning climatic states and the influence of man's activities on climatic dynamics."

Reference document:
National Climate Program Act 94th Congress, 1975-1976.

Reference quote:
congress.gov/bill/94th-congress/house-bill/12246

1978
December 7
EXXON

Exxon scientist Henry Shaw proposed that the company initiate a comprehensive research program "to assess the possible impact of the greenhouse effect on Exxon business." He argued that the company needed "a credible scientific team that can critically evaluate the information generated on the subject and be able to carry bad news, if any, to the corporation."

Reference document:
CO2 Research Proposal from Exxon Research and Engineering's Environmental Area Manager, by Henry Shaw.

1978

ENI

The Italian oil company ENI published a study by its company Tecneco, stating that: "Carbon dioxide, CO_2, is the ultimate oxidation product of fossil fuels [...] it exists in air in concentrations of about 300 ppm and only human activity increases this value by interfering with natural processes, so that above a certain threshold it becomes a pollutant."

The report by Tecneco of ENI warned that continued production and use of fossil fuels would "alter the heat balance of the atmosphere, leading to climatic change with serious consequences for the biosphere." Another section predicted that "climatic changes may occur on a regional scale due to the continued, increasing consumption of fossil fuels, and this may become a major problem by the end of the century [...] the best available data indicate that the CO_2 content of the atmosphere will reach 375-400 ppm in the year 2000; this would increase the temperature of the atmosphere by 0.5 °C." ENI's prediction was quite accurate: global warming in the year 2000 was exactly 0.5 °C and CO_2 concentrations were around 370 ppm.

Reference document:
"Ambienti e Fonti di Energia Esauribili e Rinnovabili", ECNECO, Page 7, 1978.

Reference quote:
commondreams.org/news/eni knew

1979
February 12
UN

The first "World Climate Conference" organized by the World Meteorological Organization (WMO) expressed concern that "continued expansion of man's activities on earth may cause significant extended regional and even global changes of climate." It called for "global cooperation to explore the possible future course of global climate and to take this new understanding into account in planning for the future development of human society."

The chair of the "World Climate Conference" warned that the "growing dependence" on coal could well become "the most serious threat to the world's climate." In the same year, 1979, a group of American climate scientists published the famous Charney report, which is considered a milestone in climate science for its accuracy in projecting the rate at which human-induced increases in the concentration of atmospheric CO_2 would cause global temperatures to rise.

Reference document:
"World Climate Conference", Wikipedia entry.

Reference quote:
climateconversation.org.nz/2012/05/reflections-on-a-changing-climate/

1979
August 8
EXXON

Exxon started research on how much CO_2 the ocean can absorb. The experiment began on August 8, 1979, with a state-of-the-art lab aboard the Esso Atlantic, one of the biggest supertankers of the time. Exxon's plan was to gather atmospheric and oceanic CO_2 samples from the Gulf of Mexico to the Persian Gulf.

David Shaw, main researcher on the supertanker Esso Atlantic project, said in an interview: "Our goal was to complete the carbon cycle to understand where global carbon production would end up and then make forecasts of how the system would react in the future."

Reference document:
"Exxon Believed Deep Dive Into Climate Research Would Protect Its Business" by Neela Banerjee, Lisa Song, David Hasemyer, Inside Climate News. September 17, 2015.

1979
October 16
EXXON

An Exxon internal study found that: "The present trend of fossil fuel consumption will cause dramatic environmental effects before the year 2050. [...] Recognizing the uncertainty, there is a possibility that an atmospheric CO_2 buildup will cause adverse environmental effects in enough areas of the world to consider limiting the future use of fossil fuels as major energy sources" and that "the potential problem is great and urgent."

David Shaw wrote in a November 1979 letter to Senior Vice President George T. Piercy that the research "could well influence Exxon's view about the long-term attractiveness of coal and synthetics relative to nuclear and solar energy" in a another memo he wrote "it behooves us to start a very aggressive defensive program in the indicated areas of atmospheric science and climate because there is a good probability that legislation affecting our business will be passed."

Reference document:
"Controlling the CO_2 Concentration in the Atmosphere" study by Exxon employee Steve Knisely.

Reference quote:
insideclimatenews.org/news/17092015/exxon-believed-deep-dive-into-climate-research-would-protect-its-business/

1980
February 29
API

Dr. J. Laurman told the American Petroleum Institute (API)'s Climate Task Force that "there is a scientific consensus on the potential for large future climatic response to increased CO2 levels" and that "remedial actions will take a long time to become effective."

Reference document:
Meeting Minutes from the American Petroleum Institute's CO2 and Climate Task Force. Presentation by Dr. J. Laurman.

1980

July

API

The American Petroleum Institute (API) published the booklet "Two Energy Futures: a National Choice for the 80s" in which the industry acknowledged that carbon dioxide was a "pollutant" but casted doubt on the role of CO_2 in global warming by misrepresenting what prominent scientists said at the time.

Reference document:
"Two Energy Futures: A National Choice for the 80s" by the American Petroleum Institute, Washington, DC. ISBN-0-89364-050-6.

1980
August 6
IMPERIAL OIL

An internal review by Imperial Oil, an Exxon's Canadian subsidiary, which was distributed widely to Exxon Corporate Managers, found that "it is assumed that the major contributors of CO_2 are the burning of fossil fuels" and that "technology exists to remove CO_2 from stack gasses but removal of only 50% of the CO_2 would double the cost of power generation."

The lines appeared in the report "Review of Environmental Protection Activities for 1978-1979" produced by Imperial Oil, Exxon's Canadian subsidiary, mentioning that "it is assumed that the major contributors of CO_2 are the burning of fossil fuels. [...] There is no doubt that increases in fossil fuel usage and decreases in forest cover are aggravating the potential problem of increased CO_2 in the atmosphere."

Reference document:
"Review of Environmental Protection Activities for 1978-1979" by Imperial Oil Report,
Exxon's Canadian Subsidiary.

1981
August 18
EXXON

Exxon Strategic Planning Manager Roger Cohen commented in an internal assessment of CO_2 emissions and the greenhouse effect prepared at the request of Senior VP and Director Morey O'Loughlin: "It is very likely that we will unambiguously recognize the threat by the year 2000 because of advances in climate modeling and the beginning of real experimental confirmation of the CO_2 effect" adding "whereas I can agree with the statement that our best guess is that observable effects in the year 2030 will be 'well short of catastrophic', it is distinctly possible that the Planning Division's scenario will later produce effects that will indeed be catastrophic (at least for a substantial fraction of the earth's population)."

Reference document:
Memo from Roger Cohen, Director of Exxon's Theoretical and Mathematical Science Laboratory, to Scientist Werner Glass.

1982
April 1
EXXON

An internal Exxon "CO2 'Greenhouse Effect' Summary" found that "there is concern among some scientific groups that once the effects are measurable, they might not be reversible and little could be done to correct the situation in the short term" and that "mitigation of the 'greenhouse effect' could require major reductions in fossil fuel combustion."

Reference document:
"CO2 'Greenhouse' Effect" internally distributed summary by Exxon Manager M.B. Glaser of a technical review prepared by Exxon Research and Engineering Company's Coordination and Planning Division.

1982
September 2
EXXON

The Director of Exxon's Theoretical and Mathematical Sciences Laboratory, Roger Cohen, summarized the findings of their research in climate modeling, stating that "over the past several years a clear scientific consensus has emerged regarding the expected climatic effects of increased atmospheric CO_2" and "it is generally believed that the first unambiguous CO_2-induced temperature increase will not be observable until around the year 2000" adding that "the results of our research are in accord with the scientific consensus on the effect of increased atmospheric CO_2 on climate."

Reference document:
Memo from Roger Cohen, Director of Exxon's Theoretical and Mathematical Science Laboratory, to Exxon Management Including President of Exxon Corporation's Research and Engineering, E. E. David Jr.

1982
October
EXXON

In a speech, E. E. David Jr., President of Exxon Research and Engineering Company, stated: "It is ironic that the biggest uncertainties about the CO_2 buildup are not in predicting what the climate will do, but in predicting what people will do. [...] It appears we still have time to generate the wealth and knowledge we will need to invent the transition to a stable energy system."

Reference document:
"Inventing the Future: Energy and The CO2 'Greenhouse' Effect" E. E. David Jr. Remarks at the Fourth Annual Ewing Symposium, Tenafly, New Jersey.

1985
March
SHELL

In a journal, T.G. Wilkinson, who worked at the time in the Ecology Section of Shell UK's Long Term Business Planning Unit, explored the risks posed by "energy-generated pollution." Wilkinson also considered if a precautionary approach should be adopted to prevent the "potential enormous effects on the world's climate" and considering that "the dilemma therefore remains as to whether to encourage the continued use of fossil fuels with the potential enormous effects on the world's climate."

T.G. Wilkinson of Shell wrote that the "burning of fossil fuels which have taken millions of years to form has effectively upset the balance leading to an increase in CO_2 in the atmosphere" adding that "the Greenhouse effect could lead to some melting of the ice caps and a significant change in the climatic pattern throughout the world. Whilst this will cause major adverse changes to some areas, others will benefit."

Reference document:
Journal Conservation & Recycling, T.G. Wilkinson.

Reference quote:
desmog.com/2024/01/17/new-shell-files-could-aid-climate-cases-attorneys-say/

1985
October
UN

A meeting in Villach was the culmination of a process in which three international organizations – ICSU, UNEP, and WMO – joined forces to bring an issue onto the international policy agenda. The meeting turned out to be the spark that lit the fire that awakened the world's governments, ultimately leading to the creation of the Intergovernmental Panel on Climate Change (IPCC) in 1988. In Villach in Austria, the meeting was a small gathering of climate scientists intending to discuss the results of one of the first international assessments of the potential for human-induced climate change.

Reference document:
"The origins of the IPCC: How the world woke up to climate change" from the International Science Council.

1985
December 10
WHITE HOUSE

Carl Sagan, a renowned astrophysicist, delivered a compelling and prescient speech to Congress about climate change, stating that "at the present rate, the burning of fossil fuels [...] has a variety of consequences, including redistribution of local climates and, through the melting of glaciers, an increase in global sea level." He suggested investment in renewable energy by saying "if we don't do the right thing now, there are very serious problems that our children and grandchildren will have to face."

Carl Sagan told Congress "at the present rate of the burning of fossil fuels, the present rate of increase of minor infrared absorbing gasses in the earth's atmosphere, that there will be a several centigrade degree temperature increase on the earth's global average by the middle to the end of the next century. And that has a variety of consequences, including redistribution of local climates and, through the melting of glaciers, an increase in global sea level. There is concern on a somewhat longer time scale about the collapse of the West Antarctic ice sheet and a general rise of many meters in sea level." He adds "what can be done about it? The idea that we should immediately stop burning fossil fuel has such severe economic consequences that no one, of course, will take it seriously. But there are many other things that can be done. One has to do with subsidies for fossil fuels. More efficient use could be encouraged by fewer government subsidies. [...] Secondly, there are alternative energy sources, some of which are useful, at least locally. Solar power is certainly one that might be of more general use."

Reference document:
"Greenhouse Effect. Witnesses testified on how the greenhouse effect will change the global climate system and possible solutions". December 10, 1985.

Reference quote:
theanalysis.news/carl-sagan-testifying-before-congress-in-1985-on-climate-change/

1985

December 22

NEW YORK TIMES

The first Op-Ed on The New York Times by Mobil Oil appeared in December 1985, and it was published regularly for 15 years until 2000. This form of subtle advertising was created for the first time for Mobil Oil. 'Op-Ed' means advertising on the page opposite the editorial page and it was initiated by Herbert Schmertz as a Mobil Oil executive, also known as the man who invented 'Modern PR'.

In a briefing called "Corporations and the First Amendment" that Schmertz wrote for the American Management Association in 1978, he explained why he chose the New York Times for those advertisements. He stated: "The Times was chosen because it is published in the nation's leading population, communications and business center; because it has a highly intelligent, vocal, sophisticated readership and because it reaches legislators and other government officials. In short, it was the paper most likely to reach the largest number of opinion leaders and decision makers." Schmertz also talked about the program as a great success, concluding "Mobil found that the medium worked."

Reference document:
"While the Oil is Hot" article in the New York Times, December 22, 1985.

Reference quote:
desmog.com/s3ep4-oil-slick-part-1-rise-corporate-persona/

1987

SHELL

Shell's growing understanding of the risks posed by burning its products appeared in the publication "Air Pollution: an Oil Industry Perspective." The authors of the internal Shell publication wrote that "it is feared that a further rise in carbon dioxide levels in the atmosphere could lead to a higher average surface temperature on earth, which could have far-reaching environmental, social, and economic consequences" adding that "a lot of scientific research is being done to determine which climatic changes can occur and which measures should be taken."

Reference document:
"Air Pollution: an Oil Industry Perspective" Shell Briefing Service, NR1, 1987.

Reference quote:
desmog.com/2024/01/17/new-shell-files-could-aid-climate-cases-attorneys-say/

1988

June 23

WHITE HOUSE

Dr. James Hansen, Director of NASA's Goddard Institute for Space Studies, warned the Congress that the Institute's greenhouse effect research showed that "the global warming is now large enough that we can ascribe with a high degree of confidence a cause and effect relationship with the greenhouse effect." James Hansen and other experts testified before the Senate Energy and Natural Resources Committee about the impact of global warming.

Dr. James Hansen, climatologist at NASA, stated that "altogether, this evidence represents a very strong case, in my opinion, that the greenhouse effect has been detected, and it is changing our climate now."

Reference document:
Transcript of pivotal climate-change hearing from NASA scientists. June 23, 1988.

Reference quote:
youtube.com/watch?v=UVz67cwmxTM

1988

June 24

NEW YORK TIMES

On the frontpage of the New York Times in 1988, the headline announced "Global Warming Has Begun, Expert Tells Senate", when Nasa climatologist James Hansen warned the U.S. Congress that the greenhouse effect was causing global warming.

On the front page of The New York Times, the article mentioned that "the earth has been warmer in the first five months of this year than in any comparable period since measurements began 130 years ago, and the higher temperatures can now be attributed to a long-expected global warming trend linked to pollution, a space agency scientist reported today" adding that "by burning of fossil fuels and other activities, have altered the global climate in a manner that will affect life on earth for centuries to come."

Reference document:
"Global Warming Has Begun, Expert Tells Senate" by Philip Shabecoff. Special in the New York Times, June 24, 1988.

1988

WHITE HOUSE

The U.S. Congress introduced the National Energy Policy Act in an effort to reduce emissions of heat-trapping gasses and at least four bipartisan bills were introduced in Congress, three championed by Republicans, to regulate greenhouse gas emissions.

The National Energy Policy Act of 1988 "establishes as national goals: that the amount of carbon dioxide in the atmosphere be reduced from 1988 levels by at least 20 percent by the year 2000 through a mix of Federal and State energy policies; and the establishment of an International Global Agreement on the Atmosphere by 1992."

Reference document:
Bill S.2667 - National Energy Policy Act. Introduced in the Senate on July 28, 1988.

1988

SHELL

In an internal study marked 'Confidential', called "The Greenhouse Effect", the company warned about the dire consequences: "The environment may be degraded to such an extent that some parts of earth will become uninhabitable." Shell researchers noted that "the main cause of increasing CO_2 concentrations is considered to be fossil fuel burning." It also revealed an internal Shell climate science program dating back to 1981.

The document stated that "with very long time scales involved, it would be tempting for society to wait until then to begin doing anything" adding that "the potential implications for the world are, however, so large, that policy options need to be considered much earlier. And the energy industry needs to consider how it should play its part."

Reference document:
"The Greenhouse Effect" by Shell International Petroleum, Health, Safety and Environment Division, The Hague, 1988.

1988

August 3

EXXON

The Exxon Public Affairs Manager, Joseph Carlson wrote that Exxon's position should be to "emphasize the uncertainty in scientific conclusions regarding the potential enhanced Greenhouse Effect." This was one of the first evidence of strategies of denial by Exxon and other fossil fuel companies.

Reference document:
"The Greenhouse Effect" draft written by Joseph M. Carlson. 1988.

1988
August 31
WHITE HOUSE

Vice President George H.W. Bush (Sr.), in a speech while running for President, said "those who think we are powerless to do anything about the greenhouse effect forget about the 'White House effect'; as President, I intend to do something about it."

Reference document:
Vice President George H.W. Bush (Sr.) Campaign Speech in Michigan.

1988
November 30
MOBIL

Mobil Oil's President Richard F. Tucker cited the "Greenhouse Effect" in a list of serious environmental challenges during a speech at an American Institute of Chemical Engineers national conference. In the speech (it was subsequently submitted as testimony to Congress) Tucker mentioned that action to address the greenhouse effect might require "a dramatic reduction in our dependence on fossil fuels."

Mobil Oil's President stated: "Our strategy must be to reduce pollution before it is ever generated – to prevent problems at the source" adding "that will involve working at the edge of scientific knowledge and developing new technology at every scale on the engineering spectrum. [...] Prevention on a global scale may even require a dramatic reduction in our dependence on fossil fuels – and a shift toward solar, hydrogen, and safe nuclear power. It may be possible – just possible – that the energy industry will transform itself so completely that observers will declare it a new industry."

Reference document:
"High Tech Frontiers in the Energy Industry, the Challenges Ahead" by Mobil Oil's President Richard F. Tucker. Washington D.C., November 30, 1988.

Reference quote:
huffpost.com/entry/internal-documents-show-f_b_7749988

1988
December 6
UN

The Intergovernmental Panel on Climate Change (IPCC) is formed in December 1988 by the World Meteorological Organization (WMO) and the United Nations Environment Programme (UNEP) to provide policymakers with regular assessments of the scientific basis of climate change, its impacts and future risks, and options for adaptation and mitigation.

Reference document:
"Intergovernmental Panel on Climate Change", Wikipedia entry.

1988

ENI

An issue of the Italian oil company ENI's corporate magazine Ecos – widely read by employees and executives – warned that continued use of "fossil sources" for energy would produce a "greenhouse effect that could lead to climate change with devastating effects on the entire earth's ecosystem."

Another issue of ENI's corporate magazine Ecos, from the same year, stated that as research on global warming continued "it is incumbent on us to work as of now, as far as possible, to contain the phenomenon of carbon dioxide emissions. [...] It is generally agreed that it is very important to 'buy time' so as to refine the complex prediction models and identify the most appropriate solutions. Buying time means limiting the increase in CO_2 as far as possible."

Reference document:
"ENI Knew, Too: Probe Shows Italian Oil Giant Was Aware of Climate Impacts in 1970"
by Olivia Rosane on Common Dreams. September 25, 2023.

Reference quote:
desmog.com/2023/09/24/italian-oil-giant-eni-knew-about-climate-change-more-than-50-years-ago-report-reveals/

1989
GCC

Fifty U.S. corporations and trade groups created the Global Climate Coalition (GCC) to discredit climate science and derail regulations. Its founding members included API, BP, Chevron, Exxon, Shell, Texaco, Mobil Oil, Edison, as well as GM and Ford. Until it disbanded in 2002, GCC conducted a multimillion-dollar lobbying and public relations campaign to undermine national and international efforts to address global warming.

Reference document:
"The Climate Deception Dossiers". Published on June 29, 2015.

1989
MARSHALL INSTITUTE

The George C. Marshall Institute's "Climate Change Policy" program started in 1989 in Berlin as a "critical examination of the scientific basis for global climate change policy." According to the Marshall Institute, a major part of the program was "communicating the findings to policy makers, the media, and the public policy community." Marshall Institute was part of an effort by fossil fuel companies to scientifically confuse the origins of the greenhouse effect.

Reference document:
"George C. Marshall Institute (GMI), Now CO2 Coalition" from Climate Disinformation Database, DeSmog.

1989
April
SHELL

Ged Davis, a Shell executive, warned that "global warming could challenge the very fabric of the world's ecological and economic systems" and also foresaw the possible cost for future generations if emissions weren't curbed.

In an excerpt from Shell executive Ged Davis's contribution to a 1989 report by the OECD wrote "whatever policies are chosen there will be winners and losers, and that "two groups who could bear particularly heavy costs will be: future generations who would have to live with the costs of adaptation, and [...] those in countries yet to industrialize who would face constraints on energy use. [...] How should we allocate resources between prevention and adaptation?"

Reference document:
"Energy Technologies for Reducing Emissions of Greenhouse Gases" OECD Report, 1989.

Reference quote:
desmog.com/2024/01/17/new-shell-files-could-aid-climate-cases-attorneys-say/

1989
October
SHELL

A confidential study showed that in 1989 the company was discussing the global social consequences of an increase in temperature of "considerably more" than 1.5 degrees that would displace entire populations.

The study mentioned that "the potential refugee problem [...] could be unprecedented. Africans would push into Europe, Chinese into the Soviet Union, Latins into the United States, Indonesians into Australia. Boundaries would count for little – overwhelmed by the numbers. Conflicts would abound. Civilization could prove a fragile thing." The report warned also that "many species of trees, plants, animals and insects would not be able to move and adapt."

Reference document:
Confidential Shell's "Group Planning Scenarios 1989-2010 Challenge and Response".
October, 1989.

Reference quote:
commondreams.org/news/shell-fossil-fuels-climate-1970s

1989
December 20
NEW YORK TIMES

A New York Times article reported that: "In what is considered the first major project that takes account of the changes the greenhouse effect is expected to bring, Shell engineers are designing a huge platform that anticipates rising water in the North Sea by raising the platform from the standard 30 meters – the height now thought necessary to stay above the waves that come in a once-a-century storm – to 31 or 32 meters."

Reference document:
"Greenhouse Effect: Shell Anticipates A Sea Change" article in The New York Times, December 20, 1989.

1989

GM

In a "Public Interest Report" General Motors's public relations department portrayed the field of climate science as full of uncertainties. Also in 1989, General Motors and Ford joined the Global Climate Coalition, a group that opposed efforts to reduce greenhouse gas emissions.

Reference document:
"The Climate Deception Dossiers". Published on June 29, 2015.

1990

UN

The Intergovernmental Panel on Climate Change (IPCC) published its First Assessment Report and the UN General Assembly noted the report findings and decided to initiate negotiations for a framework convention on climate change.

Reference document:
"IPCC First Assessment Report", Wikipedia entry.

1991

SHELL

Shell released a 30-minute educational video warning of climate change's negative consequences ranging from sea level rise and wetland destruction to "greenhouse refugees." It concluded that "global warming is not yet certain, but many think that the wait for final proof would be irresponsible. Action now is seen as the only safe insurance."

Reference document:
"Climate of Concern" documentary produced and distributed by Royal Dutch Shell, United Kingdom, 1991.

1991
May
ICE

The Information Council for the Environment (ICE), formed by the coal industry, launched a national climate change science denial campaign with data collection, full-page newspaper advertisements, radio commercials, a PR tour, and mailers. ICE was formed by and closely linked to fossil fuel companies and trade associations, including the Edison Electric Institute, the Western Fuels Association, and the National Coal Association. One of the Vice Presidents of the board of directors of the ICE campaign was Fred Palmer, he later became the CEO of Western Fuels and then senior vice president at Peabody Energy.

An advertisement aired is emblematic of the tone and content of ICE's messaging: "Stop panicking! I'm here to tell you that the facts simply don't jibe with the theory that catastrophic global warming is taking place. Try this fact on for size. Minneapolis has actually gotten colder. So has Albany, New York." This advertisement was created by Simmons Advertising, Inc. in 1991. The leaked ICE documents also show that the group planned to particularly target younger, lower-income women with its deceptive messages, noting that: "These women are more receptive than other audience segments to factual information concerning the evidence for global warming. They are likely to be green consumers, to believe the earth is warming, and to think the problem is serious. However, they are also likely to soften their support for federal legislation after hearing new information on global warming."

Reference document:
"Information Council for the Environment (ICE) PR Campaign", Wikipedia entry.

Reference quote:
desmog.com/information-council-environment/

1991

KOCH

The Cato Institute is established as a Koch-funded think tank, and held a seminar in Washington called "Global Environmental Crises: Science or Politics?". This was part of a decades-long effort to cast doubt on the reality of climate change. Koch Petroleum Group was a major refining and chemicals company, owning the largest oil refineries and pipeline networks that transport oil in the United States.

The New York Times described the influence of Koch: "Construction on the Koch political machine began in the 1970s, after Charles Koch took over the family company. The brothers Charles and David began funding and orchestrating a political project to restrain government power in the United States through lobbying, think tanks, and political donations. For instance the Americans for Prosperity (AFP), founded in 2004, is a libertarian conservative political advocacy group in the United States affiliated with the Koch brothers."

Reference document:
"Cato Institute", Wikipedia entry.

Reference quote:
nytimes.com/2019/08/23/opinion/sunday/david-koch-climate-change.html

1992
June 13
WHITE HOUSE

United States' President George H.W. Bush (Sr.) signed the The Rio Declaration, which was approved by the United Nations during the Conference on Environment and Development (UNCED), by name Earth Summit, held in Rio de Janeiro in June 1992.

George H.W. Bush (Sr.), on June 12, 1992, announced the following: "We have come to Rio. We have not only seen the concern, we share it. We not only care, we are taking action. We come to Rio with an action plan on climate change. It stresses energy efficiency, cleaner air, reforestation, and new technology. I am happy to report that I have just signed the Framework Convention on Climate Change." On June 13 he added: "We have signed a climate convention. We have asked others to join us in presenting action plans for the implementation of the climate convention. We have won agreement on forest principles."

Reference document:
The President's News Conference in Rio de Janeiro, June 13, 1992.

Reference quote:
govinfo.gov/content/pkg/PPP-1992-book1/html/PPP-1992-book1-doc-pg924-2.htm

1994

SHELL

Environmental Advisor of Shell, Peter Langcake, published a scientific report outlining "major developments in scientific understanding and the implications for policy formulation" that recognized "the threat of climate change as the environmental concern [...] it has the greatest significance for the fossil fuel industry."

The report recognized that many of IPCC skeptics "only raise questions or point to uncertainties rather than offer convincing alternative positions." Despite this observation, Langcake did the same, warning against "no regrets measures" that would be premature, further distort markets, and divert resources from "more pressing needs."

Reference document:
"The Enhanced Greenhouse Effect: a review of the scientific aspects". Shell Report, 1994.

1995
MOBIL

An Internal document by a team headed by a scientist Leonard S. Bernstein at Mobil Oil, which was distributed to other major fossil fuel companies, unequivocally stated: "The scientific basis for the Greenhouse Effect and the potential impact of human emissions of greenhouse gasses such as CO2 on climate is well established and cannot be denied." The document, which came to light in 2009, was leaked to the New York Times after surfacing in a lawsuit filed by the auto industry against the state of California's efforts to limit vehicles' carbon emissions.

Reference document:
"Industry Ignored Its Scientists on Climate" article in the New York Times by Andrew C. Revkin. April 23, 2009.

1995
December
GCC

The Global Climate Coalition (GCC), a fossil fuel industry group, drafted an internal primer analyzing "contrarian theories" and concluding that they do not "offer convincing arguments against the conventional model of greenhouse gas emission-induced climate change." However, a publicly distributed version excluded this section while focusing on scientific disagreement and uncertainty by citing some of those same contrarian scientists.

Reference document:
"Science and Global Climate Change: What Do We Know? What Are The Uncertainties?"
by Global Climate Coalition's (GCC). Internal Primer Draft, Prepared by GCC's Science
Technical Advisory Committee.

1996

API

The American Petroleum Institute (API) published the book "Reinventing Energy", which supported climate denial and argued for inaction by reinforcing uncertainty of the science.

Reference document:
"Reinventing Energy: Making the Right Choices" by the American Petroleum Institute (API). 1996.

1996

EXXON

An eight-page Exxon publication questioned the negative impact the greenhouse effect might have and played up the uncertainty. The introductory statement by Lee Raymond, Exxon's chairman and CEO, claimed that "scientific evidence remains inconclusive as to whether human activities affect global climate."

Reference document:
"Global Warming: who's right? Facts about a debate that's turned up more questions than answers" publication from Exxon Corporation.

1997
December 11
WHITE HOUSE

The Kyoto Protocol was adopted on 11 December 1997. Owing to a complex ratification process, it entered into force on 16 February 2005. The Kyoto Protocol was the first major international effort to slow global climate change as an agreement under the United Nations Framework Convention on Climate Change (UNFCCC). It was the world's only legally binding treaty to reduce greenhouse emissions. However, because many major emitters were not part of Kyoto, it only covered about 18% of global emissions.

The Kyoto Protocol was signed at the United Nations in New York by Acting U.N. Ambassador Peter Burleigh, saying "the United States will today sign the Kyoto Protocol, reaffirming its commitment to work with countries around the world to meet the challenge of global warming. [...] The United States signs the protocol in the firm belief that it will serve its environmental, economic, and national security goals."

Reference document:
"The Kyoto Protocol", Wikipedia entry.

Reference quote:
1997-2001.state.gov/global/global_issues/climate/fs-us_sign_kyoto_981112.html

1998

SHELL

Shell researchers wrote an internal memo about future scenarios that could harm their business. It suggested that a major storm on the East Coast in 2010 could turn public opinion against Shell and other oil and gas conglomerates, including a class action against them, while pushing governments toward strict environmental regulations and investments in renewable energy.

The prophetic memo by Shell's researchers mentioned that "following the storms, a coalition of environmental non-governmental organizations brings a class action suit against the U.S. government and fossil fuel companies on the grounds of neglecting what scientists (including their own) have been saying for years: that something must be done" the Shell researchers wrote and that "a social reaction to the use of fossil fuels grows, and individuals become 'vigilante environmentalists' in the same way, a generation earlier, they had become fiercely anti-tobacco. Direct action campaigns against companies escalate. Young consumers, especially, demand action." They determined that "only a crisis can lead to a large scale change in this world."

Reference document:
"Group Scenarios" by Shell researchers. 1998.

Reference quote:
scientificamerican.com/article/shell-grappled-with-climate-change-20-years-ago-documents-show/

1998
April 3
API

The American Petroleum Institute (API) drafted an internal strategy titled "Global Climate Science Communications Plan", a roadmap memo to develop a multi-million dollar communications and outreach plan to ensure that "climate change becomes a non-issue." The plan included obstruction, disinformation, and spreading doubts in political debates. The API's Global Climate Science Communications Team consisted of representatives from the fossil fuel industry, trade associations, and public relations firms. At the time, the team's attention was focused on derailing the Kyoto Protocol signed in 1997 and influencing the White House to make sure it would not ratify it in the future.

The Global Science Communications Action Plan stated that "victory will be achieved when [...] uncertainties in climate science become part of the conventional wisdom." The roadmap identified an array of fossil fuel industry trade associations and front groups, fossil fuel companies, and free-market think tanks to underwrite and execute the plan, including: the American Petroleum Institute and its members, Business Round Table and its members, Edison Electric Institute and its members, Independent Petroleum Association of America and its members, National Mining Association and its members, American Legislative Exchange Council, Committee for a Constructive Tomorrow, Competitive Enterprise Institute, Frontiers of Freedom, and the Marshall Institute."

Reference document:
"Global Science Communications Action Plan" draft by the American Petroleum Institute (API). April 3, 1998.

Reference quote:
ucsusa.org/resources/climate-deception-dossiers

1998

WFA

The Western Fuels Association (WFA) founded the Greening Earth Society in 1997 as a front group to spread misinformation about how increased CO_2 is making the earth greener. On November 13, 1998, the Greening earth Society released a 30-minute video titled "The Greening of the Planet Earth Continues" at the annual meeting of Basin Electric. The WFA was a not-for-profit fuel supply cooperative providing coal and transportation to utilities in the Great Plains, Rocky Mountains, Southwest, and beyond. A 1998 report by the Clearinghouse on Environmental Advocacy and Research found that the Greening Earth Society and Western Fuels are essentially the same organization.

The misleading campaign stated "expert scientists assert that CO_2 is not a pollutant, but a nutrient to life on earth" and increasing CO_2 means "faster plant growth, greater agricultural yields and improved water-use efficiency in plants. Evidence shows a picture of the ongoing industrial evolution of humankind as the greening of planet earth continues." The video, still promoted by the Center for the Study of Carbon Dioxide and Global Change "further explores issues addressed in our first video, The Greening of Planet Earth, which has been distributed to more than 30,000 people worldwide."

Reference document:
"The Greening of the Planet Earth Continues" video commercial. November 13, 1998.

1999

KOCH

Donors Trust and Donors Capital Fund are established as so-called 'dark money' groups that do not reveal their funders and are known to have supported contrarian research. According to one in-depth study, Donors Trust received millions of dollars from Koch foundations and distributed dozens of millions to groups – including the Heartland Institute, Americans for Prosperity, and the Committee for a Constructive Tomorrow – that denied the science and impacts of human caused climate change and the need to cut global warming emissions.

Reference document:
"The Climate Deception Dossiers". Published on June 29, 2015.

2000

June 1

ALEC

The American Legislative Exchange Council (ALEC), established as a platform for industry groups to influence policymakers behind closed doors, launched the "Environmental Literacy Improvement Act" to legislate the teaching of climate science denial into school curricula. ALEC's donors included General Motors, BP America, Chevron, ExxonMobil, Shell, and electric utilities Duke Energy, Entergy, and Progress Energy.

Three states pushed the ALEC bill "Environmental Literacy Improvement Act" to require teaching climate change denial in schools. As a result, Texas and Louisiana introduced education standards that require educators to teach climate change denial as a valid scientific position. A school board in Los Alamitos, California, passed a measure, identifying climate science as a controversial topic that required special instructional oversight.

Reference document:
"Environmental Literacy Improvement Act" by ALEC. June 1, 2000.

Reference quote:
desmog.com/2012/01/26/alec-model-bill-behind-push-require-climate-denial-instruction-schools/

2000
March 23
NEW YORK TIMES

ExxonMobil published an advertisement in the New York Times and the Wall Street Journal titled "Unsettled Science." The advertisement referenced a scientific paper, published in Science, claiming that the paper disputed that global warming was happening. However, after the advertisement appeared, the author of the referenced scientific paper, Dr. Lloyd Keigwin, wrote to ExxonMobil charging that the company had inappropriately and selectively used his data and exploited his research for political purposes.

A few months later, the senior scientist at Woods Hole Oceanographic Institution, Lloyd Keigwin, sent a letter to Exxon's Peter Altman, summarizing their email and phone conversations regarding Exxon's misleading use of Keigwin's study results. The letter accusing Exxon stated that "The sad thing is that a company with the resources of ExxonMobil is exploiting the data for political purposes when they could actually get much better press by supporting research into the role of the ocean in climate change."

Reference document:
"Unsettled science". The New York Times. March 23, 2000.

Reference quote:
igwin, Senior Scientist at The Woods Hole Oceanographic Institution to Peter Altman, National Campaign Coordinator for ExxonMobil. December 11, 2000.

2001
March
WHITE HOUSE

The George W. Bush (Jr.) Administration announced that it would not implement the Kyoto Protocol, the international treaty signed in 1997 in Kyoto that would have required nations to reduce their greenhouse gas emissions. Bush claimed that ratifying the treaty would create economic setbacks in the U.S. and did not put enough pressure to limit emissions from developing nations. George W. Bush (Jr.), promised to ratify the Kyoto Protocol during his presidential campaign.

A New York Times article titled "Bush, in Reversal, Won't Seek Cut In Emissions of Carbon Dioxide" on March 14, 2001, mentioned "under strong pressure from conservative Republicans and industry groups, President Bush reversed a campaign pledge today and said his administration would not seek to regulate power plants' emissions of carbon dioxide, a gas that many scientists say is a key contributor to global warming."

Reference document:
"Climate change policy of the George W. Bush (Jr.) administration", Wikipedia entry.

Reference quote:
nytimes.com/2001/03/14/us/bush-in-reversal-won-t-seek-cut-in-emissions-of-carbon-dioxide.html

2001
June 20
GCC

During State Department Undersecretary Paula Dobriansky's meeting with the Global Climate Coalition (GCC) at the American Petroleum Institute (API)'s headquarters, talking points indicated that "POTUS rejected Kyoto, in part, based on input from you" suggesting the influence of the GCC on the U.S. President's decision. The Kyoto Protocol, an international agreement committing participating countries to binding emissions reductions, was initially supported by both George H.W. Bush (Sr.) and George W. Bush (Jr.). It was adopted by the Parties to the United Nations Framework Convention on Climate Change in December 1997.

Reference document:
"Your Meeting with Members of the Global Climate Coalition", U.S. Department of State Memo and Talking Points.

2002

ALEC

By adapting fundamental principles, the American Legislative Exchange Council (ALEC), as a powerful organization of conservative state legislators and private sector representatives, aggressively opposed climate change regulations for a decade. The ALEC Energy Principles were initially adopted by the Natural Resources Task Force in 2002 and later amended at the States and Nation Policy Summit on May 16, 2008. According to ALEC.org, these principles underwent further amendment in April 2011.

ALEC Energy Principles from 2002 stated that "Global Climate Change is Inevitable. Climate change is a historical phenomenon and the debate will continue on the significance of natural and anthropogenic contributions. [...] ALEC supports affordable fuels that power growth. Mandates to transform the energy sector and use renewable energy sources place the government in the unfair position of choosing winners and losers, keeping alive industries that are dependent on special interest lobbying. [...] North America has extremely large reserves of fossil fuels. [...] Access to these resources should be expanded to provide America with low-cost and reliable energy [...] barriers limiting the use of and access to public lands must be removed."

Reference document:
"ALEC Energy Principles". 2002.

Reference quote:
alecexposed.org/wiki/ALEC_Energy_Principles_Exposed

2002
September 26
EXXON

Michael MacCracken, the former director of the National Assessment Coordination Office of the U.S. Global Change Research Program, wrote to Exxon CEO Lee Raymond in response to ExxonMobil's criticism of a U.S. climate change assessment: "In my earlier experience, arguing for study of adaptation had been a position of industry, but now when this was attempted, ExxonMobil argued this was premature. Roughly, this is equivalent to turning your back on the future and putting your head in the sand – with this position, it is no wonder ExxonMobil is the target of environmental and shareholder critics."

The letter continued: "Certainly, there are uncertainties, but decisions are made under uncertainty all the time – that is what executives are well paid to do. In this case, ExxonMobil is on the wrong side of the international scientific community, the wrong side of the findings of all the world's leading academies of science, and the wrong side of virtually all of the world's countries as expressed, without dissent, in the IPCC reports [...] to call ExxonMobil's position out of the mainstream is thus a gross understatement. There can be all kinds of perspectives about what one might or might not do to start to limit the extent of the change, but to be in opposition to the key scientific findings is rather appalling for such an established and scientific organization."

Reference document:
Letter from Michael Maccracken, Retiring Senior Scientist from the Office of the U.S. Global Change Research Program, to Exxon CEO Lee Raymond: "Re: With Regard to the ExxonMobil Facsimile on February 6, 2001 from Dr. Ag Randol to Mr. John Howard of the Council on Environmental Quality". 2002.

2002

October 21

WHITE HOUSE

Philip Cooney, Chief of Staff for the White House Council of Environmental Quality and a former lawyer and lobbyist for the American Petroleum Institute (API) with no scientific credentials, edited a "Draft Strategic Plan for the U.S. Climate Change Science Program" to introduce uncertainty about global warming and its impacts. In 2005, Cooney had to resign after being accused of doctoring scientific reports and shortly after he was hired by Exxon.

Reference document:
Markups by Philip Cooney, Chief of Staff for the White House Council on Environmental Quality, on a Draft Strategic Plan for the Climate Change Science Program.

2002

October

API

The American Petroleum Institute (API) carried out its plan to distribute curriculum materials for schools that question the established science through the National Science Teachers Association by maintaining the website "Classroom Energy!", which offers lesson plans and materials for teachers of kindergarten through high school.

Reference document:
"The Climate Deception Dossiers". Published Jun 29, 2015.

2004

BP

British Petroleum (BP) hired the public relations professionals Ogilvy & Mather to promote the term "carbon footprint". The company unveiled its "carbon footprint calculator" in 2004, with which everyone could assess how their daily life contributes to CO_2 emissions, thereby placing responsibility on individuals rather than companies and governments. Subsequently, in 2005, Ogilvy launched a large advertising campaign further popularizing the concept of a carbon footprint for individuals.

From 2004 to 2006, a $100m-plus a year BP marketing campaign "introduced the idea of a 'carbon footprint' before it was a common buzzword" according to the PR agent in charge of the campaign. The targets of this campaign were the "routine human activities" and "lifestyle choices" of "individuals" and the "average American household". In 2019, BP ran a new "Know your carbon footprint" campaign on social media. The campaign instructed people to calculate their personal footprints and provided ways for people to "go on a low-carbon diet."

Reference document:
"Merchants of Doubt" book by Naomi Oreskes, Erik M. Conway, 2010.

Reference quote:
theguardian.com/environment/2021/nov/18/the-forgotten-oil-ads-that-told-us-climate-change-was-nothing

2006

TIME

The cover of Time magazine featured a photograph of a polar bear perched on floating ice, gazing uncertainty at the surrounding sea, marking 2006 as a watershed moment in the public understanding of climate change. Just before this cover was released, the Environmental Defense Fund (EDF), a mainstream U.S. organization, launched a wide-reaching campaign. Later that spring, Al Gore released the movie "An Inconvenient Truth". Throughout the film, Al Gore framed global warming in terms of intergenerational ethics.

Environmental Defense Fund (EDF) released a TV spot in which its President announced: "Global warming has reached the point where it threatens the world we leave our children and grandchildren. This campaign is a wake-up call about the urgency of the problem." Partnering with the Ad Council, the nation's preeminent public service advertising organization, EDF sought a powerful visual symbol to make spectators feel emotionally engaged with the crisis. "We need to jolt people a bit," one of the ad's directors explained. "To think that a child today will have to bear the consequences of our apathy in years to come should be shameful and scary. If this doesn't hit everyone where it hurts, nothing will."

Reference document:
"Global Warming: Be Worried. Be Very Worried", Time magazine cover. April 3, 2006.

Reference quote:
mediapost.com/publications/article/47163/advertising-ecosystem.html

2007

CHEVRON

Chevron launched its own campaign called "Will You Join Us?" featuring television, print, outdoor, and online advertisements. The company framed itself as an environmental leader, global warming as the fault of consumers, and the solution as small changes in consumer behavior rather than a replacement of fossil fuels.

The campaign's website deflected attention from the company's role in causing climate change, stating: "Energy conservation and efficiency are seen by many as the most immediate and cost-effective ways for energy users, including the private sector and individual consumers, to reduce their carbon emissions impacts. In the advertisements, portraits of everyday Americans were emblazoned with messages including: "I will finally get a programmable thermostat", "I will use less energy", "I will leave the car at home more", and "I will replace 3 light bulbs with CFLs."

Reference document:
"Big carbon's strategic response to global warming, 1950-2020" by Benjamin Andrew Franta. 2022.

2009
August 12
API

For obstructing regulations, the American Petroleum Institute's CEO, Jack Gerard, emailed API's membership promising "up front resources" and encouraging turnout for "Energy Citizen" rallies in about 20 states. Gerard said they were "collaborating closely with the allied oil and natural gas associations" in order to "aim a loud message at those states' U.S. Senators to avoid the mistakes embodied in the House climate bill."

Reference document:
Email from the American Petroleum Institute's CEO Jack Gerard to API's Membership regarding a series of "Energy Citizen" rallies in 20 States during the end of the Congressional Recess.

2009

WSPA

The Western States Petroleum Association (WSPA), a top lobbying and trade association for the oil industry, described in a presentation the "campaigns and coalitions it has activated that have contributed to WSPA's advocacy goals and continue to respond to aggressive anti-oil initiatives in the West" including investment "in several coalitions that are best suited to drive consumer and grassroots messages to regulators and policymakers." The Sacramento-based WSPA counted among its members BP, Chevron, ExxonMobil, Shell, Occidental, and other major fossil fuel companies. Between 2009 and 2014, WSPA spent more than $26.9 million directly lobbying in California.

WSPA planned to "activate" a "significant number of campaigns and coalitions." As a presentation explained, WSPA "invested in several coalitions that are best suited to drive consumer and grassroots messages to regulators and policymakers." Among these fake coalitions were groups such as Fed Up at the Pump, California Drivers Alliance, Californians Against Higher Taxes, and Oregonians for Sound Fuel Policy. Members of Congress received forged letters opposing the bill on behalf of fake organizations including National Association of the Advancement of Colored People, American Association of University Women, American Legion, and Jefferson Area Board on Aging. The congressional investigation revealed that the fraud was perpetrated by Bonner and Associates, a lobbying firm subcontracted by a front group called the American Coalition for Clean Coal Electricity.

Reference document:
"WSPA Priority Issues". Presentation by Western States Petroleum Association President Catherine Reheis-Boyd.

Reference quote:
ucsusa.org/resources/climate-deception-dossiers

2011

API

The American Petroleum Institute (API) protested the U.S. Environmental Protection Agency (EPA)'s decision to regulate carbon pollution under the Clean Air Act. It joined a coalition of industry groups to file a lawsuit challenging the EPA's authority to regulate global warming emissions. The API's lawsuit challenged the EPA on the grounds of the same doubts about climate science.

The trade group American Petroleum Institute (API) had worked for years to manufacture misinformation, stating that "EPA professes to be 90–99% certain that anthropogenic emissions are mostly responsible for unusually high current planetary temperatures, but the record does not remotely support this level of certainty."

Reference document:
"The Climate Deception Dossiers". Published on June 29, 2015.

2012

ALEC

The American Legislative Exchange Council (ALEC) adopted legislation called the "Electricity Freedom Act" from a proposal sponsored by the climate change denial group the Heartland Institute. The legislation repealed targets for renewable energy production in place in 29 states. Between 2013 and 2015, some 65 ALEC-sponsored bills introduced in state legislatures were designed to roll back or repeal state standards requiring utilities to increase their use of renewable energy. ALEC publicly took credit for 13 states adopting resolutions "in opposition to the EPA's plans to regulate greenhouse gas emissions."

The "Electricity Freedom Act" stated that: "whereas, many renewable sources of power currently cost more than traditional electricity generation technologies, and are projected to do so for the foreseeable future; [...] Whereas, the costs of renewable energy will be borne by consumers regardless of income or circumstances."

Reference document:
"Electricity Freedom Act", American Legislative Exchange Council, 2012.

Reference quote:
progressive.org/magazine/alec-fronts-fossil-fuels/

2013
November 22
ACCOUNTABILITY INSTITUTE

Rick Heede, co-founder and director of the Climate Accountability Institute, authors a peer-reviewed study revealing that 90 producers of oil, natural gas, coal, and cement – the "Carbon Majors" – are responsible for 63 percent of cumulative industrial CO_2 and methane emissions worldwide between 1751 and 2010. The finding also revealed that just 28 companies are responsible for 25 percent of all emissions since 1965. In the following years, the institute continued to release new data, and in 2024, it estimated that 57 producers were responsible for 80% of all fossil fuel and cement CO_2 emissions since 2016.

Reference document:
"Tracing Anthropogenic Carbon Dioxide and Methane Emissions to Fossil Fuel and Cement Producers, 1854-2010" publication by Rick Heede published in Climatic Change.

CLIMATE AESTHETICS

Climate Aesthetics

Paolo Cirio explores Climate Aesthetics by delving into the realm of art that scrutinizes the social, political, and economic origins and repercussions of global warming. In critiquing misrepresentations and moralistic dimensions found in cultural works centered on climate change, Cirio advocates for a more effective Climate Aesthetics. He offers a theoretical examination of such aesthetics and provides examples of art practices and ethical considerations.

The urge to discuss the representation of climate change stems from the need to reasonably address the emotions of fear and confusion, indifference or guilt, polarization or neglect, grief and anger, and naivety and anxiety surrounding the issues of climate change. These emotions are often inadequately expressed in the realm of culture. Often they become diluted within the broader discourse on the Anthropocene, remain purely scientific, merely depict nature, or just adopt defeatist attitudes. Moreover, the scientific, historical, and political-economic aspects of climate change are frequently overlooked or misinterpreted within art and culture. The consequential misrepresentations are related to the field of ethics, as often in the art world they can be even instrumental, like in the case of green-washing, ethics-washing, and art-washing, which produce even greater confusion or negative emotions with unethical articulations.

The ethics of institutions, artists, and curators are part of Climate Aesthetics and thus can be a critical part of assessing and making works of art. However these ethics eventually form morals that might be not reasonable, and might limit forms of expression and the aims of artistic and cultural work. Alongside the ethics of representation, engagement, intention, and outcomes for artists and curators, also assessing the ethics of art production and funding is a growing concern for institutions and cultural workers that need to address climate change mitigation and adaptation. However these ethics are also often banalized, instrumentalized, or moralized, while effective actions are not considered, activists are marginalized, and key data is concealed.

The magnitude of climate change is denoted by large economic and political systems that span vast geographical and temporal dimensions. This distinctive aspect sets Climate Aesthetics apart from more general categories like ecology, sustainability, and environmentalism, which focus on pollution sources, the alteration of landscapes, ecosystem or species preservation, or the exploitation of natural resources. Instead, Climate Aesthetics considers specific climate change causes and effects to address the emotions and cognitive processes that can enhance perception and comprehension of this intricate theme.

Ethics of Climate Aesthetics

Text by Paolo Cirio. 2023.

The examination of Climate Aesthetics is to serve the creation and critique of art on climate change, which can be formed by outlining the ethics of such an aesthetics.

Climate Aesthetics reflects on the knowledge, rhetoric, and ethics surrounding climate change, focusing on social systems rather than physical systems. Employing a critical approach is essential to assess art on climate change, and to acknowledge that aesthetics is a social construct that has evolved alongside the development of human conscience throughout different historical eras, all with their own prevailing values and judgements. Climate change transforms the ethics of politics, economics, and culture from both a collective and personal perspective in everyday life. For this reason ethics are central to Climate Aesthetics, in its consideration of the ethics of representation, the ethics of modes of production, the ethics of funding, and the ethics of engagement, intentions, and outcomes. Thus, the ethics of Climate Aesthetics can be seen as an evolution of the concepts of justice and truth, conscience and knowledge in the arts. This expansion of ethics in aesthetics and global society signals a new form of humanism, one based on global consciousness of the interconnectedness of planetary forces and vulnerabilities.

The ethics of Climate Aesthetics can be considered in any artistic strategy such as figuration or abstraction, pop or conceptual art, fiction or realism, and in any medium such photography, performance, and fine arts. It is not a matter of style or genre, rather Climate Aesthetics looks at the ethics of the quality, consistency, and relevance of the social, scientific, and philosophical discourse surrounding the subject of climate change. Even if Climate Aesthetics falls mostly into the category of realism, artists also approach the representation of subjects related to climate change through speculative scenarios, expanding them through fiction; yet, all possible narratives of Climate Aesthetics are based on scientific facts, and disguising or altering them for works of art becomes a fundamental ethical question itself. Social, economic, and political realism is the focus of this aesthetics, with scientific realism as its base. Scientific truths in Climate Aesthetics connect social realities with "the aesthetic practice of realism"[1]. Similarly, the notion of "Evidentiary Realism"[2] is relevant to Climate Aesthetics and its relationship to the documentary approach. However, the inclusion of scientific, economic, or social evidence can serve as research material, and may not necessarily appear in the final work of art. In Climate Aesthetics, realism mostly deals with the relationship between social systems and climatic forces, which entail an interrelated network of factors and dynamics on a global scale that affect humanity, species, and ecosystems. Causes and effects of global warming are at the core of Climate Aesthetics, which distinguish it from other forms of art on the science of natural subsystems, environments, and materials. Climate Aesthetics does not relate directly to the notion of environmentalism and sustainability. It is necessary to distinguish Climate Aesthetics from artistic practices generally related to nature in order to provide a set of analytical tools for the making and analysis of works of art specifically addressing climate change, which ultimately contributes to the wider field of art and ecology.

By taking the science of global warming as the foundation of Climate Aesthetics, an intrinsic and consequential character of this aesthetics is the accounting of the scale of such global phenomena. The magnitude of climate change implies an exceptional geographical and temporal scale, as well as a vast economic, political, and social phenomena. Simultaneously, such expansive scales also snap back to the narrow scope of hyperlocal ecological and social crises that occur rapidly. Yet the proportions of the causes themselves remain extensive, and so aesthetic representations, significations, and discourses need to take in account the scale of comparable phenomena and relate it to the scale of social, economic, political, and personal consequences. Climate Aesthetics looks at the causes and effects of global warming, and thus origins and impacts of greenhouse emissions, which have been produced globally over the course of decades, not only from individual sources and locations within short timeframes. The scale of the causes and effects of climate change is a fundamental dimension in defining Climate Aesthetics and it challenges human cognition and perception. Even if scientific and technological tools might be able to picture and predict climate change, human emotional capacity and complexity of ethics, as well as the current political-economical and philosophical frameworks, cannot process such change. Human emotions, thoughts, and ethics surrounding climate change are not only formed using analytical science, but rather also through art that can facilitate the perception and reception of this significant epochal transition. Art can play a key role in fostering the ability to see, feel, and comprehend the scale of climate change. Particular uses of semiotics and linguistics in Climate Aesthetics can make the perception and cognition of climate change accessible through emotive, compelling, and appealing works of art. Rather than employ rhetorical devices to represent climate change with an absent referent that is vague or false, in Climate Aesthetics, effective semiotic devices and languages can enhance perception and assimilation. The accurate use of signs and significations in Climate Aesthetics refers then to the ethics of representation and the intention of a works of art.

The scale of ethical considerations implied by climate change makes ethics a central part in Climate Aesthetics. The ethics of representation, production, and outcomes of works of art are often thought of in relation to the ethics of individual responsibility, and not to governments and corporations. From the complexity of these ethics, new morals have emerged, which tend to confuse or even intentionally shift perception, thus making the use of the ethics of climate change an ethical issue itself. Defining the difference between ethics and morality in our discourse on climate change can help prevent the misuse of ethics for shaming, de-responsibilizing, or instilling paralyzing guilt. Morals around climate change mostly form by shifting the blame to individuals, or by focusing only on a single cause of greenhouse emissions. Such morals are often internalized by citizens, which the power structures then instrumentalize to evade responsibility, or to sell an alternative lifestyle. Instead of fixative morals, the science of ethics can offer more sophisticated and accurate instruments for analyzing and comparing ethics in climate change, within its magnitude of causes and effects from a political, legal, economic, and social perspective.

The ethics of Climate Aesthetics must embrace the complexity of multilayered systems around climate change, and how its social and intimate realities are created and perceived.

Notes

1. "The aesthetic practice of realism is in the intermediated space of representations where the arts, humanities, and sciences collaborate on the ongoing challenge to detail climate's history, as well as its present and future truths." From "Climate Realism" by Marija Cetinić, Lynn Badia, Jeff Diamanti, 2020.

2. "Realism in art returns through intersecting documentary, forensic, and investigative practices that contemporary realist artists utilize to bring to light the unseeable beneath the formation of our society." From "Evidentiary Realism" by Paolo Cirio, 2017.

Instances of Ethics of Climate Aesthetics

The Climate Aesthetics and its narratives look at how to express emotions, engage with audiences, explore languages, create knowledge, symbolize histories, and raise awareness about the complexity of climate change. These outcomes should be driven by genuine intentions and expressed with freedom, respect, and integrity. However, art is not neutral and often an instrument of power and even of exploitation. Often curators, institutions, and artists make use of socio-political subjects for their own benefits or sponsors. Other times subjects are avoided or misrepresented to fit mainstream narratives, through manipulation, disinformation, and censorship. Cultural producers navigating these dynamics should carefully consider the ethics of their engagement with the subject of climate change.

Ethics of Representation

Intellectual and artistic references on climate change have often focused on abstract ideas or simplistic representations. From photos of polar bears to pictures of glaciers, piles of melting ice or hot sand, it's often art about climate change that risks oversimplifying or just aestheticizing the subject.

The ethics and politics of representation concerning climate change need to be integrated into the rhetoric of narrating it. For instance, cynicism and defeatism as well as solutionism and techno-utopianism are instances of misrepresentation. Art with just solar panels, or geoengineering, carbon capture, or applying net zero, as well as art with apocalyptic or eschatologist narratives might lose sight of real scenarios, which even if grim or innovative, should refer to concrete facts and data.

On the other hand, representing climate change with only data and information or with just weather events and climate anomalies might be reductive and limit signification[1] without integrating struggles for climate justice, social inequality, and human rights. The social collapse from climate change has brought a multifaceted crisis of displacement, poverty, and irreparable loss. Addressing social justice also needs to consider the transversality and the very particular scale of climate change, which impacts not everyone in the same way, but also impacts individuals on a wide spectrum of class, race, gender, and age, throughout the world and different centuries. The audience of works about climate change might feel guilty, ashamed, scared, powerless, and hopeless, thus these climate emotions should be addressed adequately[2] and offer the possibility of empowerment through climate justice in dialogue with political movements[3]. Anger should trigger action and activism, and guilt and grief should not produce inaction and anxiety[4].

The most striking misrepresentation is the absence of cultural discourse on the actual causes of global warming. In most of the representations of climate change the focus is often only on the effects. And even when the causes are addressed the discourse remains vague on the 'Anthropocenic' cause and not how greenhouse gasses are deeply interconnected to economic and political powers[5]. Obscuring knowledge of these powers and histories inadequately addresses the subject and is unethical. Also, the frequent use of the term 'Anthropocene' misrepresents climate change, just as TJ Demos argues "The Anthropocene rhetoric frequently acts as a mechanism of universalization, albeit complexly mediated and distributed among various agents and [...] functions as a universalizing discourse: it tends to disavow differentiated responsibility (and the differently located effects) for the geological changes it designates, instead homogeneously allocating agency to the generic members of its human activities." [6]

Aestheticization of disasters and suffering from climate change is also an ethical concern, however, it's the aims that should be considered. It's a question of balancing outcomes and intentions ethically, while taking into account the sensitivity of the subject[7]. For instance, sensational climate breakdowns, mourning and grief, or monumentalizing and exposing losses are sensitive subjects that should be handled carefully and offered deep respect and consideration when represented in works of art.

Often climate change is still confused with other general questions of ecology and sustainability, like the use of recycled material, or air and water pollution. However, climate change has very particular causes and effects on a global scale which distinguishes it from other types of pollution, extinction, and deforestation. Particularly climate change is about the source of energy for industries and transportation globally, and not only in local environments.

Beside the misrepresentation, there is often non-representation of it, in which climate change is not present at all as a subject in cultural productions and presentations. Climate change in the cultural world is still rarely addressed as it's a sort of inconvenient subject. Literature has problematized its absence[8], while in contemporary art this critique is still missing. The dependence of art institutions on the market makes climate change an unsuitable subject, unless it is misrepresented. The non-inclusion of meaningful exhibitions and artworks on climate change in art programs is not only unethical but it's a sort of censorship. Even though the art world easily absorbs critiques of commodity and consumer capitalism, it seems that embarrassment and guilt have been built around the morals of feeling personally responsible and because the art market and art institutions often depend on fossil fuels sponsors and donors. However, the lack of representation of the subject and issues might still be less unethical than a misleading misrepresentation of climate change.

Ethics of Production, Funding, Outcomes, Intentions, and Engagements

Outcomes, Intentions, Engagements

When art proposes false solutions or aligns with political and corporate institutions, the intentions behind such works may be dishonest. It becomes problematic when these works are primarily intended as commodities for the art market, devoid of any meaningful social engagement, or when their outcomes are purely for entertainment or spectacle. Furthermore, if the intentions and outcomes of such works evoke negative emotions, even if intended as a form of provocation and warning, ethical concerns may arise. Additionally, works that exclusively target a limited audience, such as educational programs aimed solely at youth, could be viewed as an unethical engagement with the topic of climate change.

Funding

Exhibitions and institutions, as well as collectors and galleries might rely on capital from the fossil fuel economy. For instance, this is clearly the case of museums and art trade happening in the United Arab Emirates, of art fairs in Texas, of most of the Russian art institutions, and at times of art auctions as well. It's not only the art market, as general cultural investments by the fossil fuel industry aim to legitimize their presence in society, exert political influence, or engage in art-washing to present polluting entities as benevolent cultural philanthropists. The ethics of working with such entities and dynamics are complex, but might be unacceptable if the subject is climate change. Forms of institutional critique are necessary[9] and cultural producers that engage in such economies should be questioned.

Productions and Travels

Art producers and institutions are increasingly concerned about the 'footprint' of travel and production itself. Many policies are being put in place, often under the banner of an 'ethical code' for art institutions. While these concerns are admirable, they don't always align with the programs of these institutions and are not evenly distributed. Directors, board members, trustees, and donors often maintain engagements with fossil fuel companies and large industries reliant on large fossil fuel consumption. In contrast, artists and workers, who are already often exploited, have to adapt to ethical principles that the institution established as part of their green-washing corporate identity. Yet, the programs of exhibitions and events remain unethically instrumentalized, with inconvenient truths hidden from the audience. The morals around extensive travel in the art world present an interesting lack of rational logic, which never considers travel on behalf of the public, which includes large masses of tourists that fly from all over to visit museums. These morals extend to production practices as well, with attempts to offset the environmental impact of high energy-consuming artworks through Carbon

Credits or the use of materials that may appear sustainable, but not when placed in the larger context of the work and its display. Art institutions proudly announce these efforts, however the aims of the programs, artists, and artworks are not considered part of their ethical codes and concerns.

Notes

1. "Climate change is seen by many as having a serious perception problem; that is, a problem with regard to the manner in which it is perceived and represented. [...] The general remarks about the aesthetics of climate and climate change are political: it makes a difference whether we leave it to people to sense the changing climate or leave it to research alone. On the other hand, art – and art's approach to aesthetics – can make this and other ways of perceiving the climate crisis possible" by Birgit Schneider from "Sublime Aesthetics in the Era of Climate Crisis?", 2021.

2. "Exemplify sensitivity to the ways that visual and material qualities engender affects and create intimacy with urgent subject matter." From "Ways of Saying, Rhetorical Strategies of Environmentalist Imaging" by Suzaan Boettger, 2021.

3. "Powerful as both advocacy and art, they offer compelling models of persuasion" From "Ways of Saying, Rhetorical Strategies of Environmentalist Imaging" essay by Suzaan Boettger, 2021.

4. "We all know the apocalyptic lists of facts and figures, and the more terrifying it gets the more banal it becomes. In this terrifying banal fashion, all the news, data, etc, just pass by like any others. The only emotion they seem to evoke is the fear of the future. [...] Fear and Anxiety have become the dominant affects of our age and history shows us that fear has tended to be ground for authoritarianism. For many the response to fear is to freeze or flee, rather than to fight" by Jay Jordan of Laboratory of the Insurrectionary Imagination from "Training for the Future: Handbook", Sternberg Press, 2022.

5. "Climate Realism is offered as a reparatory concept that foregrounds the political and ecological contradictions inherent in capital's facility with energy. [...] Today we know all too well that the fossil fuel industry cannot be represented independently from the political ecology and biophysical realities of climate change, at least not if we are serious about a future disarticulated from the present." From "Climate Realism, The Aesthetics of Weather and Atmosphere in the Anthropocene", edited by Lynn Badia, Marija Cetinic, and Jeff Diamanti, Routledge, 2021.

6. "The Anthropocene is not simply the result of activities undertaken by the species Homo sapiens; instead, these effects derive from a particular nexus of epistemic, technological, social, and political economic coalescences figured in the contemporary reality of petro-capitalism." From "Art & Death: Lives Between the Fifth Assessment & the Sixth Extinction" by Heather Davis and Etienne Turpin in "Art in the Anthropocene: Encounters Among Aesthetics, Politics, Environments and Epistemologies, ed.", Open Humanities Press, 2015.

7. "Photographs of casualties and causes – hurricane-devastated homes, vast strip mines, mountain-top removal, and colorfully toxic waters – can be striking, even beautiful [...] We do have to ask if images of lethal situations are being normalized by photography. At the same time it seems counterproductive to make uninteresting images about such pressing problems. Those who choose beauty for this subject matter are most effective when they also manage to communicate the flipside, usually in series, when their choice of beauty is a conscious means to counter brutality" by Lucy R. Lippard in the essay "Describing the Indescribable Art and the Climate Crisis", 2021.

8. The missing subject of climate change in the arts can be related to Amitav Ghosh's line of thinking in "The Great Derangement: Climate Change and the Unthinkable". This comparison was also mentioned in "Everybody Talks About the Weather" by Dieter Roelstraete, Fondazione Prada, 2023. In his book, Ghosh speaks of the failure of contemporary culture to properly engage with the threat of climate change as a legitimate source for high-profile content, from the perspective of his own involvement in the literary field.

9. Among several artists engaging against fossil fuels sponsorship of art institutions, "Not an Alternative" has been the most active. They held an unauthorized demonstration at the Louvre in 2015, attacking the flagship museum's sponsorship by major oil and gas corporations ENI and Total. According to Beka Economopoulos, of Not An Alternative, "we're urging the Louvre to stop sponsoring climate chaos." toward an activist creativity directed at challenging the very structures of climate governance and finance, including the political economy of cultural institutions. Their project, The Natural History Museum organized an "Open Letter to Museums," signed by nearly 150 scientists, including several Nobel Prize winners, calling on American museums to "cut all ties with the fossil fuel industry and funders of climate science obfuscation." Generating copious press coverage, the letter was likely a major factor in oil heir industrialist David H. Koch leaving the board of New York's Natural History Museum in January 2016. Around the same time, Liberate Tate and other London-based groups won a nearly six-year campaign to compel the Tate to break off its sponsorship agreements with BP.

Climate Art Practices

"An Ethico-Aesthetic Paradigm, when art has an existential function – namely, rupture with signification and denotation – ordinary aesthetic categorizations lose a large part of their relevance. Reference to 'free figuration,' 'abstraction,' or 'conceptualism' hardly matters! What is important to know is if a work leads effectively to a mutant production of enunciation."

Félix Guattari, Chaosmosis.

Works of art can enable additional levels of perceiving, representing, and imagining climate change. However, its potential is not about the medium, such as photography, performance, digital or physical fine art, nor its about the formality of forms of representation, the focus is rather on the aims, which can be reached through several artistic strategies.

The subjects and issues addressed in the work of art can be several, such as ecological loss, mass migration, responding to extreme weather events, famine due to food supply disruption, speculative scenarios of climate justice, investigating fossil fuel companies, or financial schemes of funding, or visualizing emissions sources.

Some tactics of Climate Aesthetics

• *Raising Awareness*
Art to inform and galvanize the audience and the general public.

• *Social Commentary*
Art to examine political themes and document social, economic, and ecological conditions.

• *Social Innovation*
Art to provide social solutions and adaptation to disasters.

- *Monumentalization*

Art to remember what is lost with memorials, archives, and ceremonies.

- *Mourning*

Art for emotional support and healing through care and empathy.

- *Activism*

Art for campaigns and protests to bring change and justice.

Some strategies of Climate Aesthetics

- *Documentary*

Art including documentation of causes and effects in order to inform and keep records of events and experiences which can be used in activist, journalistic, and juridical contexts.

- *Storytelling*

Art including fiction of speculative scenarios, or that integrates the causes and effects of climate change, or is based on personal and biographical experiences.

- *Visual Art*

Art including figuration and abstraction of visual representation which can either be documentary or fiction. Any subject or issue regarding climate change can be portrayed through drawing, painting, sculpture, photography, video, imagery, data, or text.

- *Social Practices*

Art including support to vulnerable communities and individuals through social engagement, activism, or emergency response.

- *Conceptualism*

Art including economic and governance analysis, institution critique, or legal imagination, which overlays concepts, research, practices, and processes.

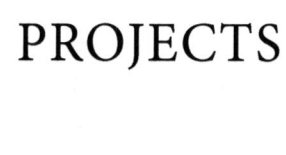

PROJECTS

Climate Legal Evidence

This series of works by Paolo Cirio consists of four graphs taken from internally commissioned studies by Shell and Exxon in the early 1980s that had assessed the effects of their greenhouse gas emissions. These studies had already precisely established that the emissions would have produced a rise in temperatures, acidification of the oceans, and many other negative effects on the climate. These documents remained undisclosed for decades and are now used as evidence in lawsuits against Shell and Exxon. In 2021, Cirio highlighted the graphs taken from these historical documents by printing them on large canvases and painting them in vibrant colors.

In 2023, a scientific paper referring to these graphs, published in the renowned journal Science, revealed that the global warming projections and models created by ExxonMobil's own scientists between 1977 and 2003 had "accurately" and "skillfully" predicted global warming due to fossil fuel combustion and had reasonably estimated the amount of CO_2 that would lead to dangerous warming. The authors of the paper concluded: "Yet, whereas academic and government scientists worked to communicate what they knew to the public, ExxonMobil worked to deny it."

Titles of the artworks in the series:
1982 Exxon increase temperature 21st Century.
1982 Exxon temperature fluctuation from 1850.
1988 Shell latitudes temperature increase.
1988 Shell ocean acidification.

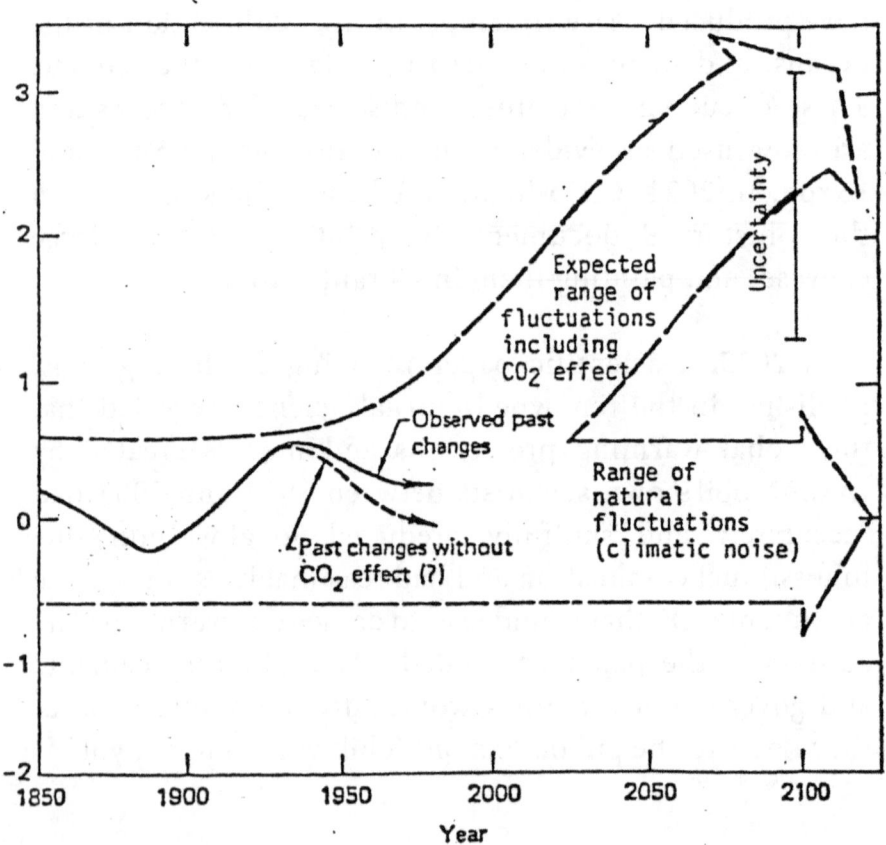

1982 Exxon increase temperature 21st Century.

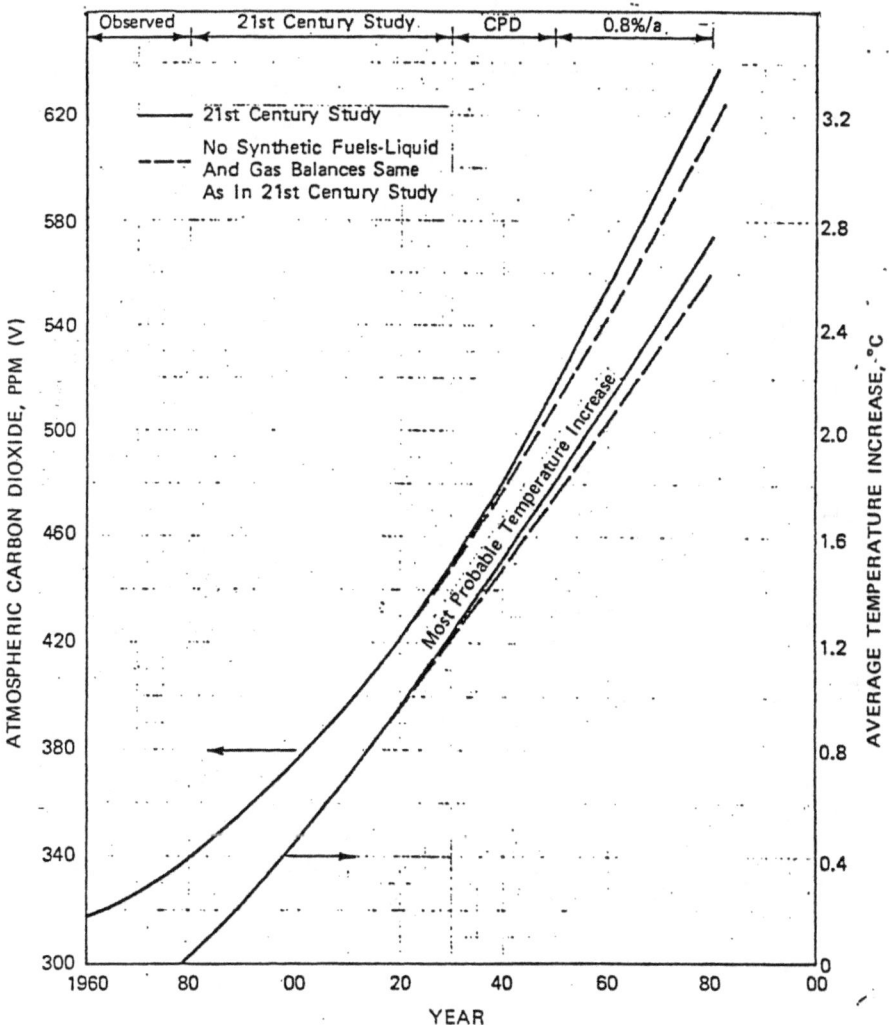

1982 Exxon temperature fluctuation from 1850.

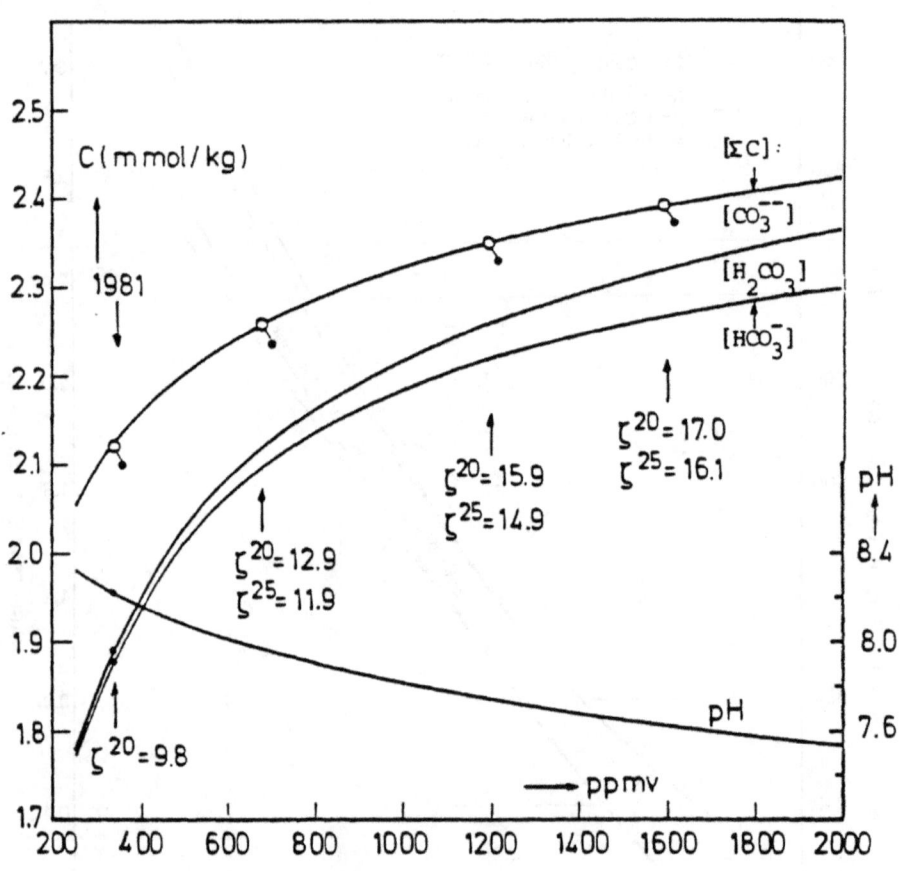

1988 Shell ocean acidification.

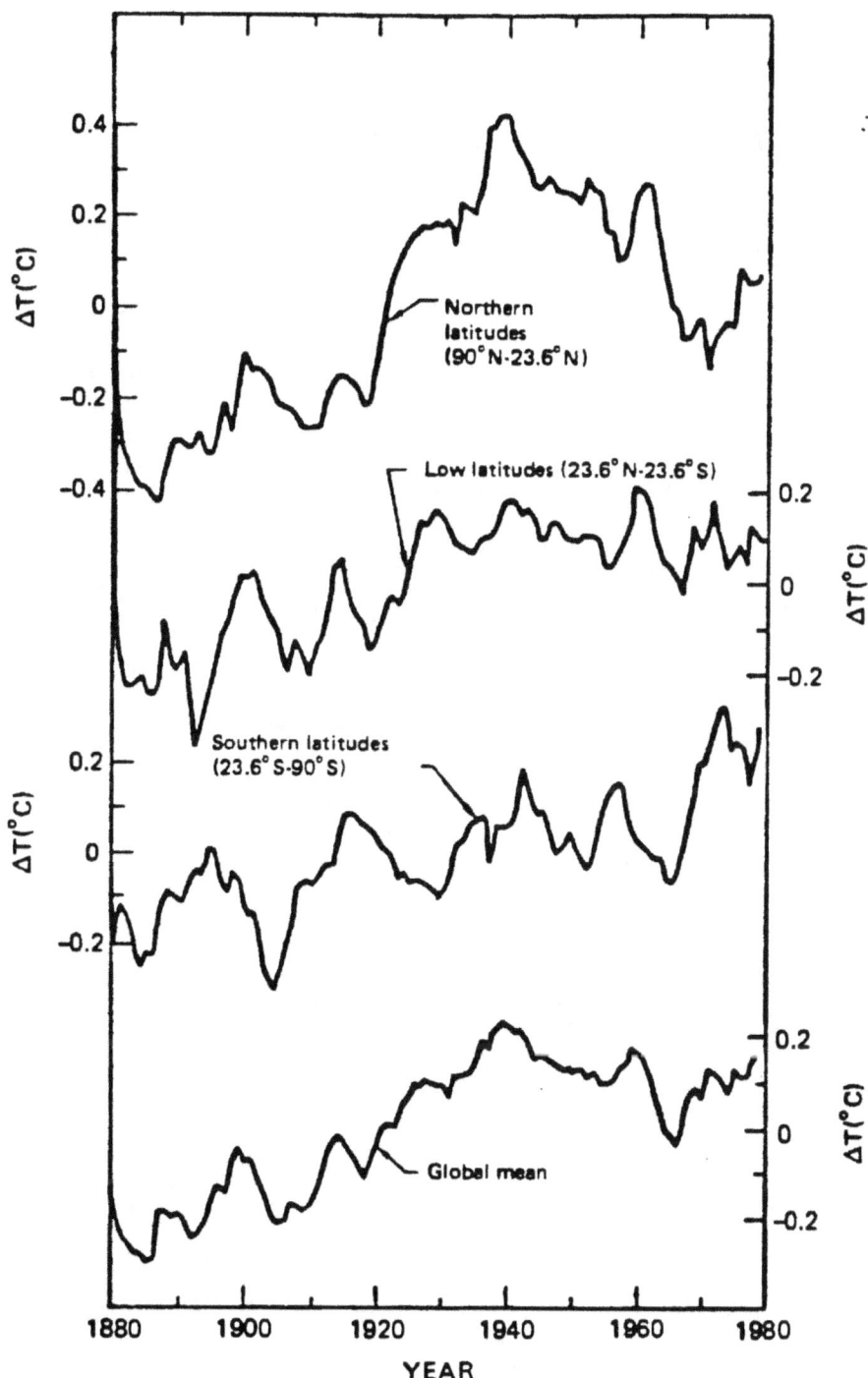

1988 Shell latitudes temperature increase.

EXXON RESEARCH AND ENGINEERING COMPANY

P.O. BOX 101, FLORHAM PARK, NEW JERSEY 07932

M. B. GLASER
Manager
Environmental Affairs Programs

Cable: ENGREXXON, N.Y.

November 12, 1982

CO_2 "Greenhouse" Effect

82EAP 266

TO: See Distribution List Attached

     Attached for your information and guidance is briefing material on the CO_2 "Greenhouse" Effect which is receiving increased attention in both the scientific and popular press as an emerging environmental issue. A brief summary is provided along with a more detailed technical review prepared by CPPD.

     The material has been given wide circulation to Exxon management and is intended to familiarize Exxon personnel with the subject. It may be used as a basis for discussing the issue with outsiders as may be appropriate. However, it should be restricted to Exxon personnel and not distributed externally.

Very truly yours,

M. B. Glaser

M. B. GLASER

MBG:rva

Attachments

H. N. WEINBERG

NOV 15 1982

1982 Front page of the Exxon's study marked as "Restricted".

THE GREENHOUSE EFFECT

SHELL INTERNATIONALE PETROLEUM MAATSCHAPPIJ B.V., THE HAGUE

Health, Safety and Environment Division (HSE)

1988 Front page of the Shell's study marked as "Confidential".

Extinction Claims

In this artwork, thousands of vulnerable and endangered species facing extinction become plaintiffs, claiming financial reparation from major oil, gas, and coal companies. Cirio aggregated data and images of species and ecosystems vulnerable to climate change, then coded an algorithm to calculate a financial compensation for them.

The results are published on the online platform Extinction-Claims.com, where the public can claim economic reparation from major fossil fuel companies on behalf of the endangered species.

The *Extinction Claims* platform contains over 40,000 species and generates simplified legal claims and petitions for each species, which can be submitted to government agencies and used for lawsuits against major polluters.

The project aims to make critical information about endangered species more accessible, while illustrating the massive scale of the crisis and holding the Carbon Majors accountable.

Cirio's artwork includes an immersive installation composed of hundreds of images of the endangered species, as well as public distribution of printed materials that provide data regarding the emissions of the respective fossil fuel companies.

Extinction Claims

Text for the project by Paolo Cirio, 2021.

This project combines the legal concept of "environmental personhood" with the "right of nature" jurisprudential theory, informed by climate change litigations, ecocide bills, and global climate treaties to give legal rights and protection to the natural world. Cirio wants to legally accuse the international oil, gas, and coal companies that deliberately emitted over 70% of all greenhouse gasses, causing extensive damage to earth's ecosystems and the species dependent on them for survival, all with the intention of covering up their crimes for decades. This project issues requests to these firms for a financial reparation which is calculated by Cirio's algorithm that integrates the economic concept of the "existence value" via contingent valuation combined with data on emissions from studies of Attribution Science.

Paolo Cirio created an equation for the algorithm that calculates a financial compensation from the Carbon Majors for the preservation of species and ecosystems. The equation considers a UN report that estimated the amount of funding necessary to avoid the degradation of the world's biodiversity. It suggests that investing only 0.1% of global GDP could help prevent the breakdown of ecosystems. Specifically, the study indicates that $536 billion per year is needed to preserve biodiversity, and an additional $203 billion per year must be spent to save forests. Cirio's equation breaks down these estimations for each species and ecosystem in the database of Extinction-Claims.com and computes them with the amount of greenhouse emissions for each Carbon Major. Moreover, existence values are captured from suggestions by participants and other coefficients are combined, such as the GDP of the country of the Carbon Majors and their active involvement in denying and perpetrating the climate crisis.

The financial reparations are designated to fund the preservation of endangered species whose natural environments are threatened by the climate crisis, while seeking legal accountability for the extermination and enormous damages done to these living beings.

Central to this project is the so-called Attribution Science, or the "effort to scientifically ascertain mechanisms responsible for recent global warming and related climate changes on Earth." In order to determine who is primarily accountable for the climate crises, related data from major oil, gas, and coal companies is found in the pivotal datasets of the Carbon Majors by the Climate Accountability Institute. These datasets are combined with aggregated data on mass extinctions from IUCN Red List to calculate how the natural world is economically and legally entitled to reparation from the companies that are knowingly causing the annihilation of species and ecosystems. Our planet now faces a global extinction crisis never witnessed by humankind. Scientists predict that more than 1 million species are on track for extinction in the upcoming decades. One of the main challenges in tackling mass extinction is the lack of public awareness and citizen agency. Most efforts in documenting the populations of different species are conducted by scientific organizations, while citizens remain ill-informed and widely unengaged, despite the urgency that is necessary to begin addressing the climate crisis and the following mass extinction.

This project aims to make these scientific issues more accessible to the general public to encourage greater participation and public discourse on these topics that are generally reserved for the scientific community. Cirio aggregated data provided from the IUCN Red List, an international union dedicated to wildlife conservation, with data from Wikipedia and iNaturalist to merge pictures and additional information on the species. The data regarding compensation for individual endangered species is formatted for the online platform with images of species with appealing design. Additionally, this material is presented as street art campaigns, installations in art institutions, and as featured articles for various press outlets. By integrating science, big data, design and art making, *Extinction Claims* directly engages the general public in understanding the scale and scope of the extinction crisis our planet faces. This project will eventually be the node for larger campaigns coordinated with environmental activists and organizations to continue action in the following years, possibly culminating with actualized legal disputes against the Carbon Majors.

The *Extinction Claims* project and campaign were launched around the time of COP26 in 2021, which stands for the 26th Conference of the Parties to the United Nations Framework Convention on Climate Change (UNFCCC). It was scheduled to take place in Glasgow, Scotland, from November 1 to 12, 2021. The project was also aligned with the largest UN Convention on Biological Diversity, scheduled for May 2022 in Kunming, China.

Posters of Extinction Claims for the Dutch Week Netherlands, 2021.

SCIENTISTS PREDICT THAT MORE THAN 1 MILLION SPECIES ARE ON TRACK FOR EXTINCTION IN THE UPCOMING DECADES.

Extinction*Claims*

October 16th – November 30th

JOIN *our campaign to* CLAIM *economic reparation from major fossil fuel companies on* BEHALF *of* THE SPECIES.
WWW. EXTINCTION-CLAIM.COM

DUTCH DESIGN WEEK 2021	NATLAB, KASTANJELAAN 500 EINDHOVERN, NL	BALTANLABORATORIES.ORG

A project presented by artist Paolo Cirio, in co-production with Baltan Laboratories and Mediamatic.

Mediamatic   ✛ BALTAN LABORATORIES

Posters of Extinction Claims for the Dutch Week Netherlands, 2021.

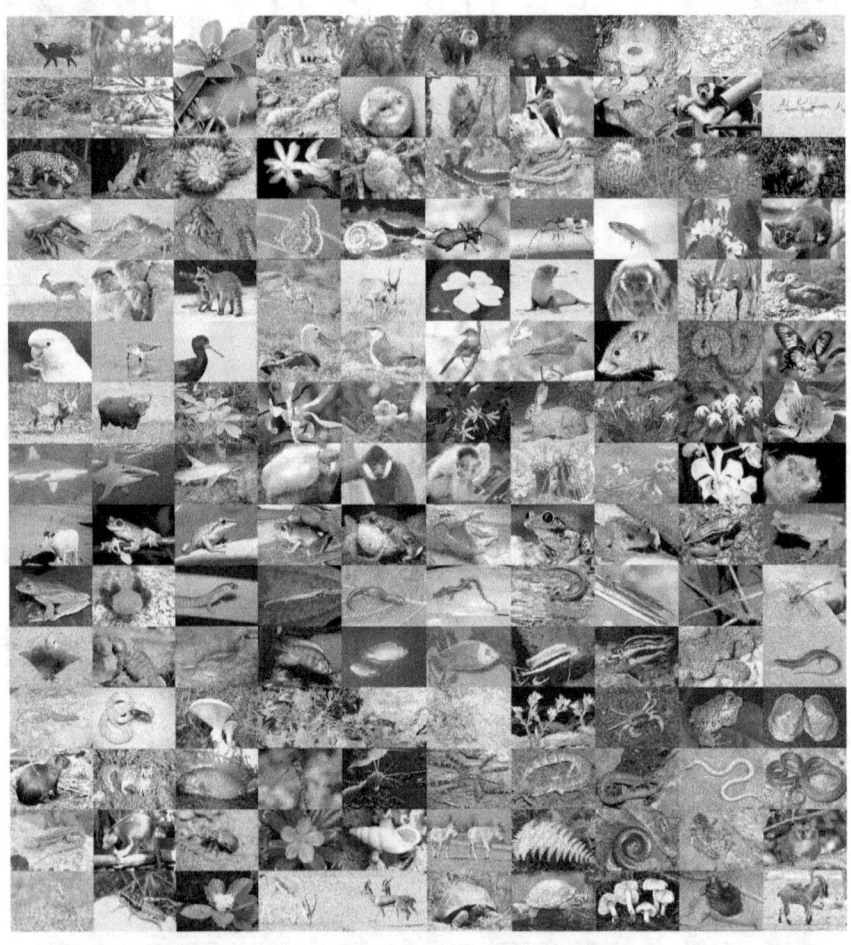

Selection of images from the database Extinction Claims, 2021.

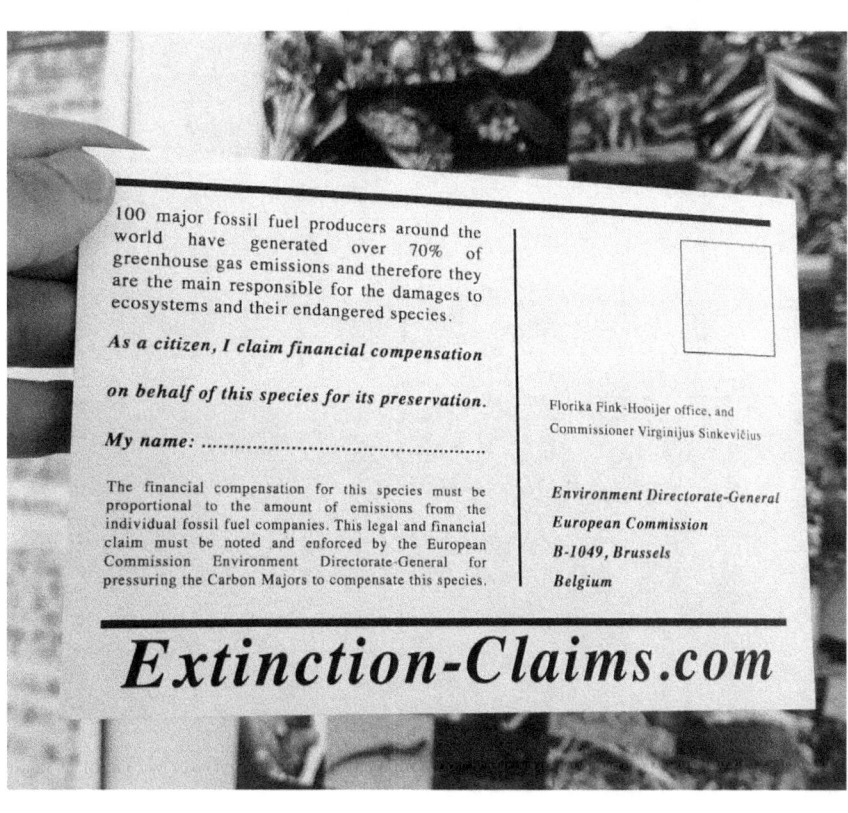

100 major fossil fuel producers around the world have generated over 70% of greenhouse gas emissions and therefore they are the main responsible for the damages to ecosystems and their endangered species.

As a citizen, I claim financial compensation

on behalf of this species for its preservation.

My name: ....

The financial compensation for this species must be proportional to the amount of emissions from the individual fossil fuel companies. This legal and financial claim must be noted and enforced by the European Commission Environment Directorate-General for pressuring the Carbon Majors to compensate this species.

Florika Fink-Hooijer office, and
Commissioner Virginijus Sinkevičius

Environment Directorate-General

European Commission

B-1049, Brussels

Belgium

Extinction-Claims.com

Postcards for the installation Extinction Claims at Fondazione Merz, 2022.

Flooding NYC Claims

Flooding NYC Claims is a project by Paolo Cirio to raise awareness about the role of fossil fuel firms in causing destructive and deadly floods in New York City. As FloodNet Artist in Residence, in 2023 Paolo Cirio developed the project *Flooding NYC Claims* to calculate compensation for New Yorkers based on flood data computed with data regarding greenhouse gas emissions by fossil fuel firms.

The project *Flooding-NYC-Claims.net* makes use of FloodNet data that is collected by sensors installed throughout New York City neighborhoods and streets for measuring the timing and depth of floods in critical locations.

The FloodNet project is a multiyear partnership between New York University, the City University of New York, and various agencies within the City of New York for developing and installing a flood sensor network across the city, and using the resulting flood data in a series of projects and services.

Flooding NYC Claims

Text for the project by Paolo Cirio, 2023.

In an era where flooding occurrences in New York City are growing more frequent and intense due to climate change driven by fossil fuel emissions, this project speculates that fossil fuel companies can be held accountable for the property damage inflicted by these floods. The *Flooding-NYC-Claims.net* website is a tool to simulate and calculate compensation. It helps determine what fossil fuel companies might owe in terms of compensation for flood-related damages and explores feasibility of pursuing legal avenues to financially aid New Yorkers who have borne the brunt of these floods. The algorithm used, merges flood data points with greenhouse gas emission data and economic damage estimates to provide a simulation of claims for reparations encompassing housing, personal belongings, health, and the various individual hardships inflicted by the flooding.

Flooding NYC Claims proposes that all New Yorkers who have been affected by a flood event should be compensated. It uses FEMA estimates for property owners and applies to everyone, in order to democratize a just compensation for all.

About the economics and science of flooding in NYC

The Mayor's Office of Climate and Environmental Justice (MOCEJ) of New York City[1] warns that climate change is causing more frequent and intense flooding due to heavy precipitation, coastal storms, and sea level rise.

These floods inflict major damage to city infrastructure, personal property and belongings of citizens, disrupting their jobs and businesses, as well as affecting their health and safety. For instance, in 2021 Hurricane Ida killed 13 people in New York City[2] alone, and 61,696 people in New York City claimed recovery funds[3] from FEMA due to the floods. In 2012, Hurricane Sandy caused 44 deaths in New York City, inundated more than 88,000 buildings, and produced an estimated $19 billion in damages[4]. Due to climate change, more powerful and destructive coastal storms are on the horizon. It is estimated that by the 2050s, a Sandy-like storm could cause nearly five times the impact – $90 billion in damage and economic loss in New York City[5].

As the climate heats up, researchers expect that there will be an increase of more extreme precipitation events, with flash floods getting "flashier," meaning that the duration of the floods will become shorter and floods will be of a bigger magnitude. These flashier floods will be more dangerous and destructive, as New York City is already experiencing.

In fact, when Hurricane Henri hit, on August 21, 2021, Central Park recorded the heaviest one-hour rainfall ever of 1.94 inches in an hour, the most rain-per-hour in record-keeping history. However, Hurricane Ida, on the night of September 1, saw 3.15 inches fall in one hour, breaking all imaginable records, with two extreme weather events just 10 days apart[6]. Weeks before Henri, the storm Elsa had also brought intense precipitation, with more than 4 inches in 24 hours[7]. Consequently, the former mayor of New York City, Bill de Blasio, established the Climate Driven Rain Response, stating "It's a different reality, a speed and intensity of rainfall that we now have to understand will be normal."[8] According to the federal government's National Climate Assessment, in the Northeast, the strongest 1 percent of storms now produces 55 percent more rainfall than they did in the mid-20th century[9]. By the end of the current century, the city could experience as much as 25 percent more annual rainfall than today, and 1.5 times as many days[10] with more than one inch of rain.

Also, floods from ocean tides will increase, and sections of the city's coastline will be subject to daily tidal flooding by the 2050s. Some low-lying neighborhoods are already experiencing chronic tidal flooding due to bigger high tides. Since 1900, the sea level in New York City has risen by about 12 inches, and is expected to continue to increase by as much as 6.25 feet by 2100[11], leading to increased frequency and intensity of coastal flooding.

Extreme rainfalls, coastal storms, and high tides severely damage New Yorkers' homes and personal belongings. Repairing damages to a home or replacing possessions can be costly, and place financial strain on homeowners, renters, and businesses, especially on low-income households that may already be struggling. New Yorkers directly threatened by flooding could more than double from about 207,000 in 2020 to 468,000 in 2080[12]. In particular, floods will hit low-income New Yorkers' apartments, exacerbating an ongoing affordable housing crisis. It has been predicted that a Sandy-like storm could flood more than 50 NYCHA social housing developments by 2080[13].

The Federal Emergency Management Agency (FEMA)[14] estimates that 1 inch of water from floods can cause as much as $11,000 in damages, based on a 1,000 square foot, single-story home. For 3 inches of water, FEMA estimates about $12,000. For 6 inches of water, loss jumps to an estimated cost of $21,000[15]. For a home of 2,500 square feet, just 1 inch of water can cost $27,000 to repair, and 6 inches of water causes damage worth $52,000. The total cost reaches $72,000 for 12 inches, $87,000 for 24 inches and $94,500 for 36 inches[16]. Certainly, the deeper the floodwater, the more it will likely cost. However, these are overly conservative estimates that do not consider population density in New York City, nor the social-economic context of those being affected by climate change. Furthermore, these home reparation costs don't consider the damages to belongings or to the jobs, health, and lives of those impacted.

Ultimately, New Yorkers' damages from flooding will not be covered by insurance, the cost will be too high. FEMA, which is funded through tax payers money, underestimates the exposure, and private insurance companies won't have enough funds to distribute. Already, homeowners' insurance is becoming unaffordable, and firms refuse to insure businesses, properties, and belongings that could be affected by climate change. Across the United States, premiums jumped 12 percent from 2021 to 2022[17], after paying out claims for about 20 disasters a year with damages of over $1 billion[18] in recent years. In many cases, insurers are pulling back in areas considered high-risk for climate disaster[19], leaving citizens to state-backed insurance plans. Yet, both private and government-backed insurers are undercapitalized for dealing with the potentially massive disasters[20] of the coming years.

In contrast, fossil fuel companies staked record profits for decades, knowing the consequences of their products, dismissing projections of the damages they would bring, and axing any alternative renewable energy source.

Therefore, fossil fuel companies must compensate New Yorkers for the increasing floods in New York City.

How the claims are calculated

The calculation for the compensations is based on a proposal to compensate everyone living near a flood event. Starting from the rough FEMA estimate of $11,000 for one inch of flooding in a 1,000 square foot home, the equation computes the depth of water with the estimates for damages and reparation costs by the square foot. It then adds it to the amount claimed, and ultimately computes the sum using the percentage of greenhouse emissions from each fossil fuel firm. The final estimates reflect amounts that ideally all New Yorkers affected by a flood should receive, even if they don't own properties. Other parameters to take into account would include the income and assets of claimants, while claims for health and death are not considered based on the depth of the floods.

Notes

1. Climate Resilience New York City - climate.cityofnewyork.us

2. NYC Flooding and Hurricane Ida Live Updates (September 3, 2021) - nytimes.com/live/2021/09/03/nyregion/nyc-flooding-ida

3. NYC's Denial of Financial Claims for Hurricane Ida Flooding - thecity.nyc/housing/2022/8/16/23308728/nyc-denies-every-financial-claim-for-hurricane-ida-flooding

4. Urban Transformations and Climate Change - urbantransformations.biomedcentral.com/articles/10.1186/s42854-020-00014-w

5. Coastal Surge Flooding Challenges in New York City - climate.cityofnewyork.us/challenges/coastal-surge-flooding/

6. Impact of Hurricane Ida on New York City - nytimes.com/2021/09/03/nyregion/nyc-ida.html

7. Beyond Flood Risk Mapping: Insights from Resilience Quarterly - resiliencequarterly.com/beyond-flood-risk-mapping/

8. Live Updates on NYC Flooding from Hurricane Ida (September 3, 2021) - nytimes.com/live/2021/09/03/nyregion/nyc-flooding-ida

9. Hurricane Ida's NYC Flooding Live Coverage (September 3, 2021) - nytimes.com/live/2021/09/03/nyregion/nyc-flooding-ida

10. Extreme Rainfall Challenges in New York City - climate.cityofnewyork.us/challenges/extreme-rainfall/

11. Addressing Coastal Surge Flooding in New York City - climate.cityofnewyork.us/challenges/coastal-surge-flooding/

12. A Decade After Sandy: Revealing New York's Climate Future Through Flood Maps - npr.org/2022/10/29/1131608305/a-decade-after-sandy-hurricane-flood-maps-reveal-new-yorks-climate-future

13. Examining NYC's Climate Future: Insights A Decade After Hurricane Sandy - npr.org/2022/10/29/1131608305/a-decade-after-sandy-hurricane-flood-maps-reveal-new-yorks-climate-future

14. Federal Emergency Management Agency (FEMA) Official Site - fema.gov

15. Flood Insurance and the National Flood Insurance Program (NFIP) Factsheet - fema.gov/fact-sheet/flood-insurance-and-nfip

16. Flooding Statistics and Insights - finder.com/flooding-stats

17. July 2022 Home Insurance Pricing Report - policygenius.com/homeowners-insurance/home-insurance-pricing-report-july-2022/

18. Billion-Dollar Weather and Climate Disasters: Summary Stats - ncei.noaa.gov/access/billions/summary-stats

19. State Farm's Insurance Policy Changes Due to Climate Risks - theguardian.com/us-news/2023/jul/05/state-farm-stopped-insuring-california-homes-due-to-climate-risks-but-it-shares-lobbyists-with-big-oil

20. How Climate Change Is Changing Insurance Markets - Senate Budget Committee Hearing - budget.senate.gov/hearings/risky-business-how-climate-change-is-changing-insurance-markets

Drowning NYC

In the spring of 2010, Cirio began work on the *Drowning NYC* project, an experimental fiction piece that addressed rising sea levels due to global warming and their impact on New York City's urban population. This project served as a source of inspiration and reflection on climate change justice in New York City, highlighting emerging economic and social dynamics driven by rising sea levels. The narrative was conveyed through actors and narrative devices over the Internet and in specific public spaces within selected Manhattan neighborhoods, with a particular focus on the Lower East Side, especially Stuyvesant Town along the East River waterfront.

The story revolved around a company that Cirio branded, the Future Water Proof Corporation firm, and its CEO Michael Meyer planning to exploit the rising sea levels around New York City. Jason Gompers, a young streetwise man, believed that gentrification resulting from the corporation's new developments to adapt to rising sea levels would force his neighborhood's residents to leave. He took it upon himself to investigate the corporation and established Future Climate Change Fighters' cells to oppose the CEO's plans. The narrative explored the potential impacts of adapting and mitigating the effects of global warming on the city's future, particularly in gentrified and impoverished neighborhoods. This project relied on early data about sea level rise in New York City.

In 2009, the Mayor of New York City released climate change projections specific to the city, developed by the New York City Panel on Climate Change (NNPC), which included scientists, legal experts, insurance professionals, and waterfront management specialists.

For this story, in 2010, Cirio envisioned Future Climate Change Fighters as a social movement of concerned teenagers, emphasizing the role of global politics in the fossil fuel economy in their manifesto. Almost as if predicting what was to come, in 2012, the devastating superstorm Sandy hit New York City and in 2018, Greta Thunberg's initial climate strike contributed to the formation of the Fridays for Future high school movement.

In recent years, extensive waterfront redevelopment has been undertaken throughout New York City to address the increasingly frequent and destructive floods. However, this still leaves residents in lower-income neighborhoods at risk of devastating flooding.

FUTURE CLIMATE CHANGE FIGHTERS NYC

Manifesto of Future Climate Change Fighters

We have clear pragmatic points, not bullshits like turning off the bathroom lights or banning cars on Sunday. Painting everything green is not going to save the world. Politicians, firms and media try to feign responsibility - identifying themselves as environmentalists - to win over citizens. Meanwhile the real causes of global warming stem from a lack of regulations and general irresponsibility from big industries.

What F.C.C.F. wants in order to stop global warming right now:

- *Free public transportation for anyone. We want more trains for free. We want infrastructures that diminish the number of flights and cars. This is possible and will cost less than adapting cities to the devastating effects of sea level rise.*

- *Use local goods instead of relying on wasteful shipments. We want goods produced close to consumers, we reject the dizzying transport of stuff around the world, which causes harmful CO_2 emissions and damages the world economy.*

- *Decrease energy waste by the industry complex. Energy recycling and designing efficient electric devices can save much electricity, making enough renewable energy for the whole nation and eliminating the need for new coal and nuclear power plants.*

- *Eliminate plastic consumer products and establish more efficient recycling services. Many materials and recycled items can replace plastic consumer goods. This will have the effect of reducing oil usage and will obsolesce the harmful practice of burning garbage. We want to ban the production of useless plastic stuff in the US.*

- *We want to boycott and call for an embargo against all the countries that don't cut CO_2 emissions. By regulating the market of demands, we can force nations like China and India to develop sustainable production standards.*

- *Judge those responsible for global warming as criminals against humanity. Impose substantial fines on oil corporations like Exxon, Shell, BP, as well automotive manufacturers and other harmful organizations, pressuring them to reinvest their money in clean public transportation infrastructures.*

People of the world must have the power to regulate the short-term private interests of corporations and nations that aren't showing concern for the health of the whole planet. This not fictional, this is real shit!

October 2010.
Jason Gompers,
Future Climate Change Fighters promoter.
(just a kid from the last avenue on the Lower East Side)
http://www.facebook.com/pages/Climate-Change-Fighters-NYC/116705608386337

PS: F.C.C.F. fights Michael Meyer as a symbolic enemy. He represents the growing camp of 'climate change vultures' worldwide. These are a group of entrepreneurs who aim to adapt to, and capitalize on climate change rather than mitigate it. Locally, Meyer screws us in our daily lives, in our houses, and throughout our neighborhoods. We need to change this culture of putting profits over people and nature.

We need to move the collective imagination toward the right path.
We need to avoid disasters not adapt to them.
It is not too late to stop global warming!

Flyer for the Climate Change Fighters distributed in Lower East Side, Manhattan, 2010.

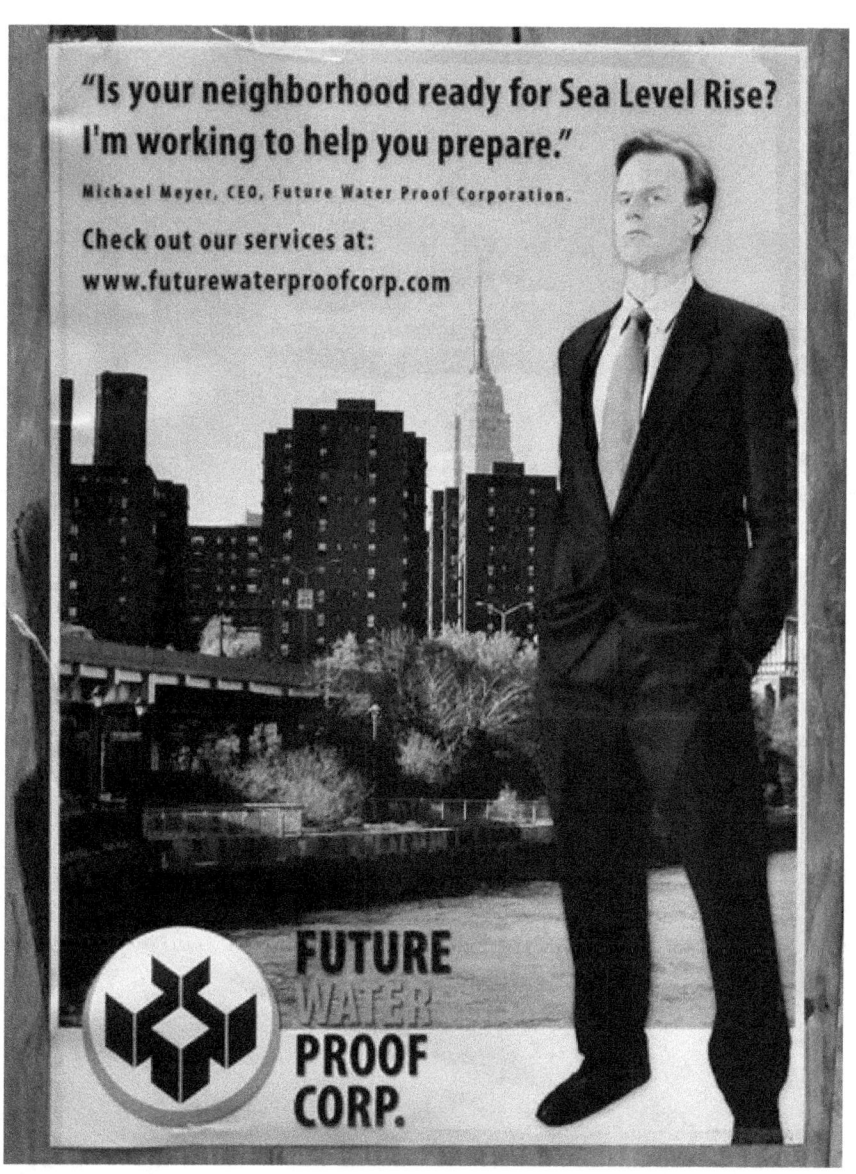

Poster for the Future Water Proof Corp posted in Lower East Side, Manhattan, 2010.

V-A-C Foundation

Intervention, Venice, 22 April 2022.

The intervention by Paolo Cirio in Venice consisted of posting spoof posters that inform on the ties between the Russian gas industry and the founder of the art institution V-A-C Foundation, Leonid Mikhelson, who is supported directly by Vladimir Putin.

Paolo Cirio wrote an investigative short essay on the V-A-C Foundation, its museum in Venice, and its direct ties with the Russian gas firm Novatek. This text was featured in his poster campaign, which took place throughout Venice during the opening days of the Biennale Arte 2022.

With the war in Ukraine and the intensifying climate crisis, it is necessary to acknowledge how these two issues are connected: a fossil fuels war waged not only for dominance over energy resources but also against the restraint of fossil fuels extraction. Emphasizing these issues aims to enrich the cultural perceptions about this war. Thus, culture and art should play a role in challenging these perceptions, instead of being part of an economy based on fossil fuels money, which produces war and climate cataclysms.

Between 'institution critique' and 'protest art', Cirio points at art institutions engaged in green-washing and art-washing while being directly connected to horrifying abuses of human rights and environmental destruction. Cirio calls art institutions, their supporters and curators to remove themselves from these perverse art economies based on fossil fuels. If today the conflict is from Russia, tomorrow it could be from China, Saudi Arabia, or even Texas, because any connection with any fossil fuels producers and polluters will inevitably be about the military and social wars of the future.

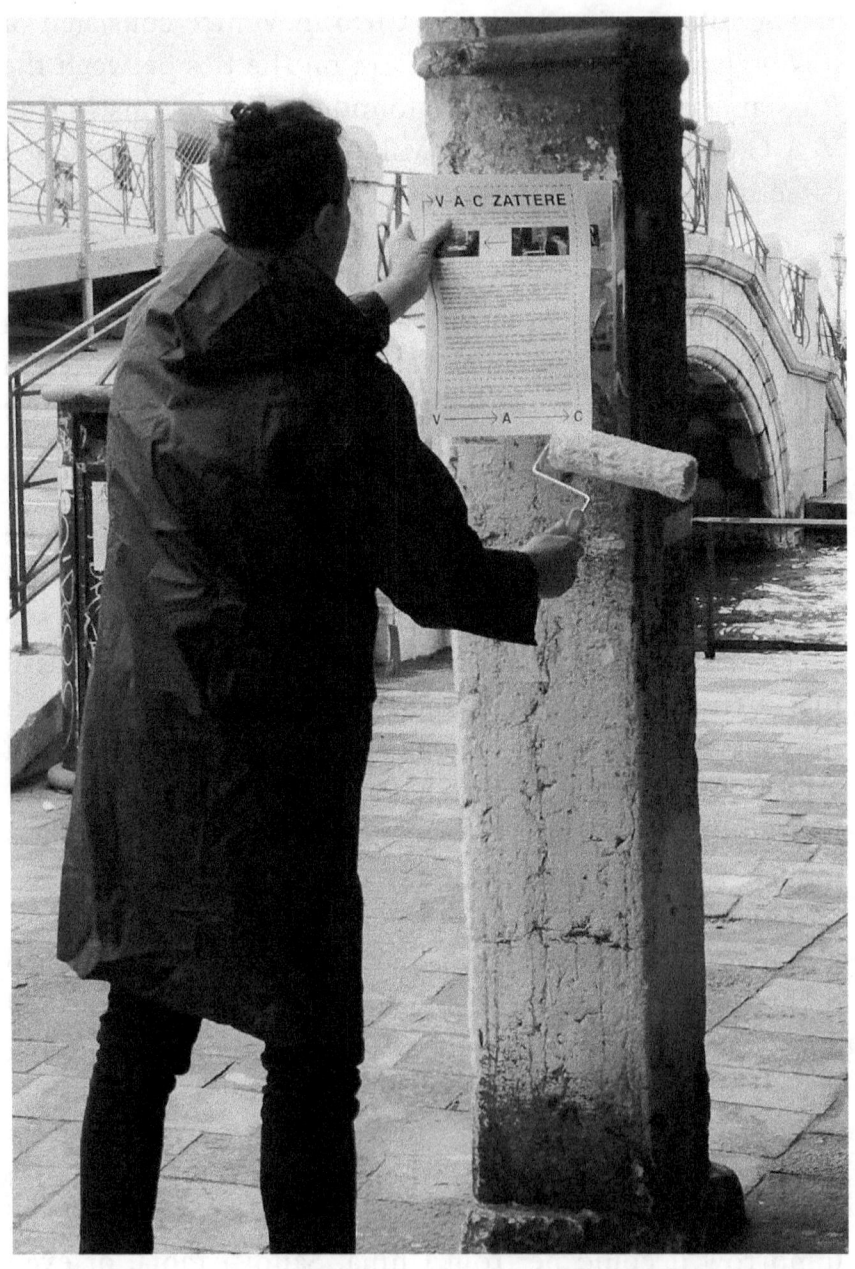

Paolo Cirio pasting posters against V-A-C Foundation in Venice, 2022.

→V–A–C ZATTERE

The Venice V-A-C Zattere contemporary art foundation is funded by Leonid Mikhelson, who has close ties to the Kremlin and is chief executive of Novatek, Russia's largest private gas group.

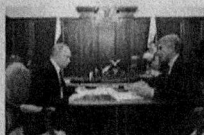 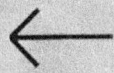 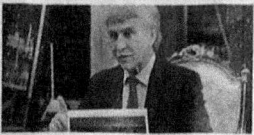

In May 2021, Vladimir Putin had a meeting with Leonid Mikhelson and had agreed to license his company Novatek to the expansion of LNG Gas facilities in the Arctic in order to increase its output target for 2030 by about 20% — as much as 70 million tons.

Additionally, Russian authorities promised to make new nuclear ice-breaking vessels, Rosatomflot, available to the company to deliver LNG Gas cargoes from Yamal and Gydan Russian peninsulas to Asia and the Pacific all year round through the so-called eastern route via Russian Arctic Seas by 2023.

The new $21 billion Arctic LNG Gas project will likely double the demand of LNG Gas over the next 15 years and raise Russia's share in the global LNG Gas market up by 20 percent.

This Arctic expansion in extraction of LNG Gas will be responsible for a considerable amount of Greenhouse gas emissions. LNG Gas is one of the most emission intensive resources.

A carbon budget for limiting the global average temperature rise to 2°C requires most global fossil fuel reserves to remain in the ground, which includes half of the gas reserve currently available.

The tycoon Leonid Mikhelson is not currently subject to sanctions, though his company Novatek is. According to Forbes, Leonid Mikhelson is Russia's richest businessman.

V-A-C FOUNDATION, DORSODURO 1401, 30123 VENICE

V ⟶ A ⟶ C

Posters against V-A-C Foundation in Venice, 2022.

AFTERWORD

Afterword

Around 2019, I felt a sudden sense of urgency about something I had already known for a long time, having researched the subject ten years before. Even so, I couldn't help but follow my instinct. As an artist, my primary resource is the feeling that guides me towards the right projects to pursue.

The feeling that invaded me was coming from plants, from rain, from heat. Something was changing, and much more rapidly than what I'd studied years before. However, it wasn't my research on climate change that alarmed me, it was the feeling.

After all, I grew up on a farm, closely following the seasons to oversee the growing of plants, and to make sure fruits were healthy, as part of an ecosystem of insects and birds living alongside bacteria and fungi. The symbiosis of ecosystems is something I understand not as a biologist, but intuitively. Also as a farmer, I have felt the economic and social consequences of too much or too little rain, not from the standpoint of economics, but rather from the traumas of ancestral famines, from hardship that spanned centuries and generations.

It's this feeling that sparked me to dive into a new research project on climate change. Around 2019, I began to gather new data, publications, contacts, and news articles. I didn't know what I was about to rediscover after having taken a ten-year hiatus from this field of research. At first, I was amazed by new developments. Science had progressed, providing new data about polluters, implementation of climate policies, possibilities for new renewable energy, and there were now digital tools capable of mapping the entire planet's atmospheric gasses, quantifying and comparing them within the context of climate change. Climate movements were powerful, exciting and energetic, with their protagonists ranging from children to elderly, and the concerns bridging generations and surpassing ideological barriers, as they were politically transversal.

However, the deeper I dug, the grimmer it got. The new data available pointed out that the solutions were actually much more diminished than previously thought. Meanwhile, climate disasters were accelerating and unfolding right before my eyes. I personally experienced the heatwave in Europe in 2003, the major hurricane in New York in 2012, and the wildfires in California in 2018. But it was the year 2020 that marked a new spiral of temperature increases, mega droughts, and flooding that started breaking records every month, and every year. Meanwhile a global pandemic destabilized and delayed political and social efforts to mitigate the climate crisis, and new wars started reshaping the geopolitics of energy production.

And yet, the saddest discovery was noticing the discrepancy between data, facts, and knowledge. In the cultural field, in the arts as well as education, there was a lack of understanding surrounding the whole issue. It was often reduced to addressing the health of polar bears or bees, or how mushrooms could save us. All noble discourses, but ones that ignored that climate was a much bigger destructive force that was thought, that the causes were much different than our personal lifestyles or natural phenomena, and finally, that the proposed solutions were not effective. There is an established history, there is scientific support, and plenty of data, but I also discovered that even in 2023 I still had to piece everything together, reading tons of articles and searching for books, and that experts were also struggling to get exposure. It was clear that the level of opacity on climate change was greater than expected.

This is what I aimed to explore with my research, art making, and theoretical reflection. However, such unmasking and demystification is something the cultural world fears. Somehow I am undertaking a kamikaze mission, not due to personal risk, as is the case in other projects of mine, but because I will face censorship born of fear, lies, and ignorance from museums, curators, outlets, journalists, universities, professors, and researchers. Sadly, there is a great aversion toward speaking the truth about something that is changing the world as we know it, being the most destructive event of the past one million years.

Bibliography

"Against the Anthropocene: Visual Culture and Environment Today" by TJ Demos, Sternberg Press, 2017.

"Climate Realism, The Aesthetics of Weather and Atmosphere in the Anthropocene" edited by Lynn Badia, Marija Cetinic, and Jeff Diamanti, Routledge, 2021.

"The Routledge Companion to Contemporary Art, Visual Culture, and Climate Change" edited by T. J. Demos, Emily Eliza Scott, and Subhankar Banerjee, Taylor & Francis, 2021.

"From Big Oil to Big Green: Holding the Oil Industry to Account for the Climate Crisis" by Marco Grasso, MIT Press, 2022.

"Ending Fossil Fuels. Why Net Zero is Not Enough" by Holly Jean Buck, Verso, 2021.

"On Fire: The (Burning) Case for a Green New Deal" by Naomi Klein, Simon & Schuster, 2019.

"How to Blow Up a Pipeline: Learning to Fight in a World on Fire" by Andreas Malm, Verso, 2021.

"White Skin, Black Fuel: On the Danger of Fossil Fascism" by Andreas Malm and the Zetkin Collective, Verso, 2021.

"After the Apocalypse" by Srećko Horvat, Polity, 2021.

"Art in the Anthropocene: Encounters Among Aesthetics, Politics, Environments and Epistemologies, ed.", Open Humanities Press, 2015.

"The End of Nature" by Bill McKibben, Random House, 1989.

"Merchants of Doubt" by Naomi Oreskes, Bloomsbury, 2011.

"Climate Crisis and the Global Green New Deal" by Noam Chomsky and Robert Pollin, Verso, 2020.

"The Sixth Extinction: An Unnatural History" by Elizabeth Kolbert, Holt, 2014.

"Climate Justice" by Mary Robinson, Bloomsbury, 2018.

"Climate Matters, Ethics in a Warming World" by John Broome, Norton, 2012.

"The Ethics of Climate Change: Right and Wrong in a Warming World" by James Garvey, Bloomsbury, 2008.

"A Perfect Moral Storm. The Ethical Tragedy of Climate Change" by Stephen M. Gardiner, Oxford, 2011.

"Barricading the Ice Sheets" by Oliver Ressler, Camera Austria, Graz, 2020.

"Training for the Future: Handbook" by Florian Malzacher, Jonas Staal, Sternberg Press, 2022.

"Everybody Talks About the Weather" by Dieter Roelstraete, Prada, 2023.

"Environmental Politics" by Andrew Dobson, Oxford University Press, 2016.

"Environmental Law" by Elizabeth Fisher, Oxford University Press, 2017.

"Environmental Ethics" by Robin Attfield, Oxford University Press, 2017.

"The Climate Deception Dossiers" by the Union of Concerned Scientists, 2015.

"Smoke, Mirrors & Hot Air" by the Union of Concerned Scientists, 2007.

"Documentary Evidence" by the Climate Integrity, 2019.

"A Crack in the Shell: New Documents Expose a Hidden Climate History" by the Center for International Environmental Law, April, 2018.

"Big Carbon's Strategic Response To Global Warming, 1950-2020" by Benjamin Franta, Stanford University, 2022.

"Dirty Pearls: Exposing Shell's hidden legacy of climate change accountability, from 1970 to 1990" a project for which researcher by Vatan Hüzeir, 2023.

"I bugiardi del clima" by Stella Levantesi, Laterza, 2020.

"Non c'è più tempo" by Luca Mercalli, Einaudi, 2018.

Acknowledgments

Paolo Cirio's research on climate change was supported by Strasbourg University's Lethica Institute, New York University's Tandom School, Hamburg University's City Science Lab, European Commission's Joint Research Centre in Ispra, Baltan Laboratories in Eindhoven and MediaMatic in Amsterdam. The creation of the of artworks were supported by Giorgio Persano Gallery in Turin, and NOME Gallery in Berlin.

Curators supporting and inspiring Paolo Cirio include Blanca de la Torre, Olga Mink, Olga Subirós, Cristina Goberna, Claudia Schnugg, Freo Majer, Marco Baravalle, Marco Scotini, Francesco Martone, Andrea Lerda, Marina Guida, Giulia Saya, Franz Fischer, Diego Mantoan, Shaul Bassi, Fabrizio Panozzo, Alessia Gervasone, Daniel Borselli, Mariasolo Garacci, Carolina Fernández-Castrillo, Dieter Roelstraete, Miranda Massie, Camille Pene, Alice Audouin, and Stefano Vendramin.

The scientific research was supported by Marco Grasso, Stella Levantesi, Marco Armiero, Ivan Novelli, Veronica Dini, Luca Mercalli, and Gaby Langendijk.

Artists supporting and inspiring Paolo Cirio include Amy Balkin, Oliver Ressler, Igor Grubić, Terike Haapoja, Paul Miller, Andres Chang, Sue Montoya, Joana Moll, Elizabeth Henaff, Tega Brain, Beka Economopoulos, Jason Jones, Jay Jordan, Mike Bonanno, Hans Haacke, and Lucy R. Lippard.

Copyrights

ISBN FOR DISTRIBUTION
978-1-4461-9158-3

9 781446 191583